Therapy Games

Creative Ways to Turn Popular Games into Activities

(Manage Anxiety Depression and Stress Improve Communications Skills and Self-esteem Through)

Donald Stewart

Published By **Darby Connor**

Donald Stewart

Therapy Games: Creative Ways to Turn Popular Games into Activities (Manage Anxiety Depression and Stress Improve Communications Skills and Self-esteem Through)

ISBN   978-1-998927-55-5

No part of this guidebook shall be reproduced in any form without permission in writing from the publisher except in the case of brief quotations embodied in critical articles or reviews.

Legal & Disclaimer

The information contained in this book is not designed to replace or take the place of any form of medicine or professional medical advice. The information in this book has been provided for educational & entertainment purposes only.

The information contained in this book has been compiled from sources deemed reliable, and it is accurate to the best of the Author's knowledge; however, the Author cannot guarantee its accuracy and validity and cannot be held liable for any errors or omissions. Changes are periodically made to this book. You must consult your doctor or get professional medical advice before using any of the suggested remedies, techniques, or information in this book.

Table Of Contents

Chapter 1: Mental Health for Kids

Our mental fitness essentially influences our cutting-edge health. You, as a discern, can do masses to sell your infant's highbrow fitness. Nurturing and compassionate care may also help the social and emotional improvement of your teen, giving them the statistics and talents had to live a happy, healthful, and green lifestyles. Your infant's social, highbrow, and bodily capabilities increase as they start university. They are gaining the ability to offer an purpose at the back of activities and precise their emotions extra.

As children flip their hobby from home to the outdoor worldwide, friends and social norms turn out to be extra vital. Your youngster is developing independence and a mind-set of duty with the aid of spending greater far from home. Some older children will begin the puberty approach and undergo severa mood modifications.

Achieving cognitive and mental milestones, obtaining tremendous social capabilities, and studying to deal with worrying situations are all part of growing up mentally well. Mentally wholesome youngsters are happier and extra able to thriving at domestic, in university, and of their cultures.

Serious deviations from how children usually take a look at, behave or control their feelings are intellectual problems in youngsters. These deviations create distress and make every day responsibilities hard. Many youngsters periodically go through tension, fear, or act out in disruptive approaches. The teenager may be identified as having a mental illness if their symptoms are severe and chronic and restriction their capacity to perform at play, at home, or at college.

1.1 Importance of Mental Health

Overall health relies upon on highbrow fitness. Mental problems are prolonged-lasting and frequently chronic fitness troubles that might last the whole lot of someone's existence. Kids with intellectual problems can also additionally enjoy problems at home, in schoolwork, and in making buddies if early assessment and treatment aren't acquired. Mental ailments can also obstruct a child's ordinary growth, critical to problems that very last into adulthood. Ensuring youngsters attain developmental milestones, know-how what to do if there are troubles, assisting effective parenting strategies, and improving get entry to to care are all factors assisting children's highbrow health.

As they increase, kids go through diverse emotions, in conjunction with tension, disappointment, worry, stress, aggression, joy, and desire. Children are likely to experience fantastic concerning themselves once they manage robust feelings or manipulate their panic in attempting or emotional activities.

Mental nicely-being includes accurate physical fitness. Being lively promotes nicely health, elevated electricity, self-guarantee, stress manipulate, and sound sleep to your teen.

Here are a few tips for retaining your child wholesome and physical in shape:

•Encourage your circle of relatives to eat nicely through offering nutritious meals.

•Encourage your teenager to participate in various sports and physical sports.

•Trying new subjects is beneficial on your strength and fitness. Children also can advantage from feeling awesome approximately themselves. As they observe new skills, it may moreover assist youngsters feel authentic about themselves.

•Ensure that your infant gets the rest they require. Your toddler may be better capable of deal with stress and a hectic time desk with sufficient sleep.

1.2 How Mental Health Affects Overall Performance of Kids

Serious deviations from how youngsters generally study, behave or control their emotions are intellectual troubles in children. These deviations create misery and make every day duties hard. Many youngsters periodically undergo anxiety, fear, or act out in disruptive tactics. The youngster may be suspected of getting a intellectual state of affairs if their signs and signs and symptoms are severe and persistent and intrude with their functionality to carry out at play, at domestic, or at university.

Student typical performance might be hampered via way of highbrow health issues that impair their degree of power, hobby, reliability, intellectual capability, and optimism.

According to research, unhappiness and tension co-taking area can pork up the link between depression and poorer grade element averages. The desire to move away school has moreover been associated with melancholy.

Mental troubles are long-lasting and often persistent fitness issues that might remaining everything of a person's existence. Kids with highbrow troubles may additionally experience issues at domestic, in training, and in making friends if early assessment and remedy aren't furnished. Mental illnesses can also hinder a little one's regular increase, main to problems that very last into maturity.

1.Three Main Issues That Cause Mental Illness in Kids

Children revel in u.S.A.And downs often, which has an impact on how they revel in and act. However, there are instances while youngsters do now not 'bounce back from the lows, which begins offevolved offevolved to harm wonderful factors in their lives. It may additionally furthermore mean that a toddler is experiencing intellectual health issues.

It's important to talk collectively at the side of your youngsters and sooner or later are looking for professional help if you see any mental infection symptoms and signs in your infant and that they persist for longer than some weeks.

The infant's behavioral and emotional warning symptoms may additionally have a facts of tantrums. For instance, youngsters may also additionally moreover act defiantly or aggressively regularly, regularly cries out of worry or fear, well-knownshows incredible signs of unhappiness or disappointment, turns into especially disturbed while eliminated from atmospheres, are pretty unhappy at the same time as you are away or withdraws from social conditions.

Kids moreover begin acting in approaches which aren't suitable. For example, they will have issues focusing, has problem staying although, or is stressed. They moreover have physical indicators together with Kid possesses trouble ingesting or sleeping. Headaches, stomachaches, nausea, and special physical sensations are examples of bodily pain that doesn't have a scientific clarification.

You can also check your little one if they may be no longer acting nicely, as wellknown, no longer being capable of wholesome in at university or get along aspect one of a kind children and refusing to attend social gatherings like birthday celebrations.

1.4 Depression in Children

Many youngsters fear and fear the worst, and they from time to time ought to even feel depressed and hopeless. During various degrees of life, excessive concerns may moreover moreover surface. For instance, even though they'll be stable and well cared for, toddlers frequently precise incredible pain approximately being separated from their parents. Although issues and fears are commonplace in children, tension or depression can be the purpose of chronic or excessive sorts of fear or disappointment. They are internalizing problems thinking about that thoughts and emotions are the precept symptoms and signs and signs.

There are diverse signs and signs and symptoms of young people depression. Due to signs and symptoms being misdiagnosed as normal emotional and intellectual modifications, the infection frequently is going unreported and untreated. Early clinical studies centered on "masked" melancholy, in which a little one's gloomy mood modified into manifested with the aid of appearing out or irrational conduct. While this once in a while happens, specially in greater younger kids, many children additionally display signs of melancholy or despair, just like depressive adults. Sadness, a enjoy of helplessness, and a depressed mood are youngsters' fundamental symptoms and symptoms of melancholy.

1.Five Types of Mental Disorders

Anxiety conditions

Anxiety issues encompass generalized tension problems, commonplace fears, precise obsessions, worry ailments, obsessive-compulsive syndrome (OCD), and put up-demanding tension contamination. If untreated, anxiety problems might also additionally have a tremendous unfavorable influence on a person's each day life.

Children's emotional and behavioral troubles

Oppositional defiant illness, hobby deficit hyperactivity contamination and conduct sickness are commonplace behavioral issues in youngsters. Therapy, schooling, and remedy are all feasible varieties of treatment for positive highbrow fitness conditions.

Eating Disorder

Obesity, social and emotional issues, and one among a type binge eating troubles are examples of ingesting issues. Both women and men can be afflicted with the aid of consuming issues, which can have number one intellectual and somatic repercussions.

Trauma-Related Anxiety Disorder

Post-stressful stress syndrome afflicts everybody and may be brought on with the beneficial useful resource of any terrible incident.

1.6 Talking with Teenagers About Mental Health

Teenagers want to understand that they may be accountable for their well-being, communicate out once they begin to be aware issues and deal with others with understand. Many highbrow sicknesses start in children, yet many teenagers do now not get the assist they require proper now quickly. It's not important to be that way. Teenagers can deal with demanding situations more all at once in the occasion that they art work to preserve superb intellectual properly-being and are looking for for help early.

Make talking about intellectual health a normal problem count. When your adolescent needs to talk, be there and display interest. Do now not be hesitant to initiate a conversation with the useful resource of posing a question. When you notice that your teen is underneath stress or is expressing a number of awful thoughts about themselves or the situation, you may moreover deliver up intellectual fitness.

These are the primary points to deliver to teenagers.

• The more you emulate them, the extra effective they may be. Everybody has highbrow fitness. Everyone's fitness, especially intellectual health, is crucial.

• When you've got were given top highbrow health, you could address stress better. It can be tough to be ok with your self while you do not feel top approximately yourself.

• It's regular to have horrific days as a human. Everybody on occasion memories a terrible day or possibly a terrible week. When we stumble upon tension, remorse, loss, or unique distressing situations, it isn't uncommon to experience depressed, harassed, or irritating.

•Speak up and ask for assist if you are involved approximately your highbrow fitness. Doing so lets in you to address issues earlier than they get worse or appreciably have an effect on your existence.

Chapter 2: Ways to Boost Your Kid's Mental Health

As dad and mom, it's far our responsibility to ensure our youngsters get assist at each stage of boom. There are various techniques that mother and father can use to assist their little one's highbrow fitness, no matter the fact that expert involvement can be important at the same time as children are struggling to manipulate substantially with life—modeling powerful coping mechanisms.

Practicing coping mechanisms at home might also teach your kids wholesome strategies to deal with their emotions. You can exercising these skills together with your infant or assist them learn how to use them by myself. For example, deep respiratory, the usage of strain balls, developing paintings, and going on walks are all effective coping mechanisms.

Children regularly revel in behavioral changes as they improve through numerous developmental degrees. However, if you discover that your little one is being greater reclusive or far off from their buddies, family, or each day sports, it could suggest that they may be going thru some factor that they can't cope with on their non-public. Inform your teenager that you are there for them and prepared to help them but they want via checking in with them.

Your toddler wants to understand that they're capable of come to you with any problem and that you could reap them and listen to them with love and assist. The opportunity that they may come to you when they have a problem can be improved via way of informing them of your presence to guide and be aware of them without judgment.

A little one's lifestyles might likely emerge as pretty disturbing or stressful because of uncertainty about each day schedules. Developing a important sample at domestic, inclusive of a plan for every day food or a weekly movie night time time, might also moreover offer your baby a few consolation and quiet. In addition, having smooth obstacles can assist mother and father and youngsters experience tons less annoyed via letting them comprehend what is anticipated of them at domestic.

The maximum beneficial element you could supply a infant is an environment in which they revel in valued and loved. They experience extra solid and cushty of their houses when you endure in mind that they're conscious that they may be supported regardless of what they do.

Children revel in listening to compliments and being recommended they did an awesome project. A toddler's sentiments of delight and self assurance can final prolonged in the occasion that they realise they did a few aspect properly. Additionally, encouraging children to duplicate an motion via giving them terrific reinforcement is commonplace.

2.1 Spend Quality Time with The Kids

The bodily and intellectual fitness of the children who spend greater time with their mother and father is observed to be better than individuals who do not spend an lousy lot time collectively. So, spending extraordinary time collectively along side your youngsters is crucial for each their well-being and your non-public.

Here are some trustworthy recommendations for spending pleasant time together along with your kids:

•Keep each day touch collectively along with your infant. Any interaction together along with your kids, whether or not or not in person in advance than paintings or college or thru leaving a piece observe of their lunchbox, is good sized and treasured.

•Every day, tell your baby you like them. Tell your youngster why you cherish and care approximately them.

•Establish a normal ritual, which incorporates choosing and studying a quick e-book before bed.

•Your praise will assist to beautify positive conduct.

•Together, put together dinner and consume it. It promotes verbal exchange at a few level within the circle of relatives and encourages cooperation.

•Schedule a time to have interaction in an hobby collectively collectively along with your youngster; allow them to pick out out it. Such as making matters, baking, having family recreation nights, and so forth.

•It may be only for a few minutes; play at the facet of your teenager.

•Make your little one laugh thru telling jokes. Laughter is a wonderful way to beautify emotional nicely-being.

•Spend a half of of-hour disconnecting from generation and clearly speakme and listening to your teenager.

Establishing huge relationships collectively in conjunction with your kids is vital, and doing so can be a sincere daily goal. They will experience lengthy-lasting consequences from doing in order they come to be contributing human beings in

2.2 Listen Carefully to What Kids Say

Your child income communication skills for every you and one of a kind human beings while you figure on enhancing your courting at the side of your infant. In addition, it'll assist beautify your bond collectively with your infant through demonstrating recognize for their reviews and emotions.

Here are a few ideas:

•Schedule time to speak and listen to one another. An top notch possibility to do this could be within the route of circle of relatives meals.

•When you and your infant communicate, turn off your telephones, laptop structures, and TVs. It demonstrates your undivided interest to the communique or engagement.

•As you bypass about your day, speak about not unusual subjects. When extremely good or hard issues get up, discussing if you and your infant are used to doing so can be less complicated.

•Be inclined to talk approximately all emotions, which encompass anger, pleasure, frustration, fear, and fear. It aids on your little one's 'feelings vocabulary' improvement.

•Show which you are paying interest through manner of using the use of your frame language. Face your child and appearance them in the attention, for example. If your baby enjoys speakme whilst sporting out play, you may show them which you are paying attention with the aid of turning to stand them and shifting in near.

•Keep a watch constant for your toddler's frame language and facial feelings. It is vital to apprehend what is being stated similarly to virtually hearing the phrases spoken while listening.

2.Three Be Friends with Your Kid and Praise Their Efforts

Focus on praising college students for his or her artwork to acquire their objectives in preference to figuring out them as obviously extraordinary youngsters. A pupil's development can be substantially impacted thru praise. Children are stimulated, encouraged, and inspired the usage of it. Students discover ways to understand the connection among their try and results at the identical time as praised for running diligently on a project or placing aside time every night time time to examine.

Children adore compliments and interest. Children can, however, spot faux flattery. It can be easy to praise a more younger character in reality to decorate their conceitedness. For the child to apprehend the reward, be as precise as you may.

2.Four Teach Them to Be Disciplined

Children can look at properly out of your calm phrases and deeds. Show your youngsters the way to act through placing an example.

Set boundaries. Make certain your youngsters can obey your smooth and normal hints.

Explain the repercussions if kids do no longer behave forcefully but calmly. Tell her, for instance, that you may placed her toys away for the rest of the day if she does not tidy them up. Be organized to act proper now after. You need not provide in by using returning them after a brief whilst. Never deprive your little one of some issue they need, like a meal.

Before helping with the solution, allow your youngster end the story. Watch for instances on the identical time as terrible conduct is repeated, which incorporates even as your youngster feels inexperienced with envy. Instead of certainly enforcing punishment, have a verbal exchange collectively at the side of your youngster about this.

Pay attention to them. Attention is the handiest weapon for punishment on the grounds that it is able to both deter horrible behavior and beef up right behavior. Keep in mind that each one children choice their dad and mom' interest.

Observe them doing nicely. Children should advantage statistics of to apprehend each first-rate and horrible behavior. Therefore, observe fantastic conduct and get in touch with it out, worthwhile accomplishments and sincere efforts.

2.Five Set Reasonable Expectations

Children always observe through on expectancies. Your children will commonly stay up in your expectancies if you have excessive expectancies for them. Conversely, they'll come up with little or no when you have low expectations of them.

As a determine, it's crucial to strike the appropriate stability amongst having excessive expectancies on your child and now not setting them up for failure or placing an excessive amount of stress on them inside the occasion that they fall short of them. You can wonderful recognize your toddler and set the proper policies for him in this sensitive balancing act. Consider your infant's skills, hobbies, and regions of energy and susceptible element. Then, adapt your expectations to the individual.

Clearly outline prolonged-term expectancies and set up checkpoints along the way. Make excellent your infant is aware what to prepare for inside the future.

2.6 Teach Your Kid to Have a Positive Outlook

Being dad and mom, we want to educate our kids the way to understand life's fantastic and ugly elements with a more cheap and balanced attitude. To accomplish this, but, we want to test our attitudes and assist our youngsters in developing an super outlook on the arena.

According to specialists, maximum individual traits are innate, however our surroundings have an impact on a few. If your infant has a bent to be gloomier than optimistic, you should replicate in your outlook first. The most large have an impact on on a baby's worldview comes from their dad and mom and one of a kind caregivers. Children mimic what they see; therefore, if they see you react cheerfully to a miserable circumstance, they will learn how to do the identical. Therefore, your conduct right away affects how your teen perspectives the arena.

2.7 Highlight Their Strengths

Each infant has each strengths and weaknesses. Concentrating for your infant's shortcomings and areas that require improvement is ordinary. However, it is as critical to recognize your infant's capabilities.

You also can assist your toddler in growing self-attention and arrogance via using being aware about these strengths. Additionally, you may paintings on difficult troubles in a good deal a good deal much less demanding methods through the usage of utilizing your talents. Recognizing your infant's strengths may be made easier thru the use of following the ones steps.

Think about many instructions of strengths. Strengths is probably large or small, apparent or unnoticeable. Then, use the tick list to determine your infant's areas of electricity.

Consider what draws your youngster. Sometimes as your little one pursues interests, strengths emerge. Find out how you could encourage your teen to comply with their pastimes and broaden new abilties.

2.Eight Involve Them in House Chores

The best location to workout self-sufficiency is at home. Children supporting with domestic responsibilities foster a piece ethic, promote independence, and perhaps a worthwhile revel in. Additionally, youngsters frequently like seeing the distinction a few elbow grease makes in dusty wardrobes and grimy restrooms. Children who assist out the own family regularly experience valued and useful.

2.Nine Encourage Your Youngster to Build Good Relationships with Others

Relationship-constructing is forming emotional bonds with others constructed on take transport of as actual with and intimacy that begin at starting. Children examine themselves and others via their relationships. The capacity to explicit emotions successfully and to recognize the emotions of others are stipulations for growing outstanding, healthful relationships. Teach kids appropriate techniques to precise their rage, which encompass making an indignant portray, sprinting within the backyard, or throwing a pillow at the floor.

2.10 Boost Physical Activity

Encourage your infant to have interaction in as a minimum 60 minutes of physical hobby daily, collectively with unstructured active play to organization sports activities. Here are a few techniques for doing this: Take own family walks or engage in active video games as a circle of relatives to embody exercising into your ordinary routine.

Bring children to internet web sites where they can be energetic, like community baseball, basketball courts, or parks.

Encourage your toddler to be curious about new sports activities by using supporting their participation in physical sports.

Make exercise exciting. Any thrilling interest to your infant, whether or not scheduled or not, can be taken into consideration beneficial.

2.Eleven Teach Them Relaxing Techniques

The more suitable manner to deal with the hassle is to educate children to apprehend the symptoms and signs and symptoms of the problems as they begin to experience them. Parents and instructors ought to apprehend a way to understand kids experiencing excessive strain and anxiety degrees. Because of this, younger individuals can observe strategies to control symptoms earlier than they purpose damage.

Using images to depict fear, infection, sorrow, and special sensations assist teach youngsters a way to end up privy to the ones and particular unfavourable emotions.

2.12 Be A Good Example for Your Kids

Setting an extremely good example in your children is one method to instilling appreciate and notable manners. It want now not be a exceptional deal because of the truth a small gesture can advocate masses. According to specialists, your kids are constantly searching at the entirety you do. According to specialists, your children are constantly gazing the entirety you do.

They will begin to be aware your splendid behavior even as you do it within the the the front of them, and they will even imitate it. Kids will begin to study your outstanding conduct while you do it in the the front of them, and they'll even imitate it.

2.Thirteen Ask Them to Practice Gratitude

Being grateful and pleased with some thing you've got already have been given is the definition of gratitude. Simply taking a 2d to famend our advantages can make us happier, extra comfortable, and hold a extremely good mind-set. An interesting location of research has been fostering thankfulness in youngsters and young human beings.

According to 3 research, cultivating thankfulness improves social, bodily, and emotional nicely-being. Stronger interpersonal talents, greater consider in others, decrease strain degrees, a higher ability to overcome limitations, diminished feelings of envy, and better sleep first rate are only some examples. However, we have to first recognize gratitude to teach and promote it in youngsters and teens in truth

Chapter 3: Fun and Entertaining Activities for Kids to Boost Self-Esteem

A toddler's intellectual improvement might be hampered through manner of low vanity. It will boom with sports like Camping, Bonfire Circles, Tell Tale Gameplay, and some sports activities sports that foster closeness. The boom of kids and younger humans is based upon on fostering sturdy senses of self esteem and self belief. It lets in human beings to increase greater emotionally strong and deal with pressure and troubles in life more effectively.

Many youngsters warfare with low shallowness. It can give up end result from their surroundings or the difficulty they have got encountered inside the past. Nevertheless, they take this stuff seriously and suppose negatively of themselves due to the fact their minds are however growing.

Keeping your teenager busy with fun sports can resource in growing vital abilties and growth self-assurance of their abilities.

3.1 Self-Esteem and Its Importance for Kids

Children who are assured in themselves are greater willing to try new topics. They are extra willing to offer it their all. They are thrilled with their skills. Kids who enjoy assured can cope with errors better. Even in the event that they initially fail, it encourages youngsters to attempt all all over again. Children that have better vanity perform better of their academic, private, and social lives.

Children who lack self-self assurance doubt their skills. They won't participate within the occasion that they revel in like others will not receive them. They may want to permit others to mistreat them. They must battle to propose for themselves. They may with out problems give up or give up altogether. When they make a mistake, lose, or fail, youngsters with low arrogance have a hard time handling it.

Learning to clearly be given flaws whilst selecting to revel in your self permits expand vanity. Every time a teenager engages in effective exchanges the usage of encouraging terms, their feel of self esteem will increase. Building a little one's self-self guarantee in their functionality to manipulate their lifestyles is critical.

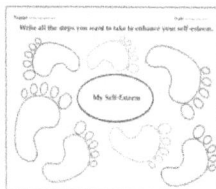

three.2 Ensure They Know Your Love Is Unconditional

There are clean strategies to show your little one which you take care of them, and whilst a teen feels loved via their mother and father, the whole thing of their lifestyles improves. Make superb your youngster is aware of which you are considering their opinions. Everything may not have to be a test or a analyzing hobby. Find strategies to revel in your self with each other.

Although telling your baby you like them is important, do not reduce rate the importance of physical contact in reaffirming your love for them. Asking kids for his or her evaluations shows them which you recognize what they have got to say and that you care about what they've got to mention, whether or no longer or now not the question is wherein to get takeout for lunch or some factor broader much like what they reflect onconsideration on transferring.

three.Three Practice Positive Self-Talk with Them

Positive self-speak is a coping method that empowers children to reframe their views, fosters resilience, and elevates vanity. Happy self-talk has a good buy more to do with social-emotional studying than genuinely encouraging a powerful outlook. Positive self-speak instructs the thoughts to appearance strengths, areas for development, and justifications for trying once more.

Constructive self-speak can appreciably modify mind and feelings. Positive self-talk can in the long run help children feel an entire lot less forced, have higher vanity, be greater inspired and characteristic higher intellectual and physical health. Parents, teachers, and counselors can all play a giant component in assisting children and teens in locating their unique voices for optimistic self-talk.

three.Four Give Them Age-Appropriate "Special Tasks" To Help You Out

Give them greater assignments further to housekeeping to make them sense useful, geared up, and responsible. Using the adjective "unique" encourages children' self-self perception even greater. Being your assistant as you cook, looking after your puppy or younger sister even as desired, or, for a completely younger little one, clearly garb himself are all examples of particular duties. Give kids extra assignments in addition to housekeeping and schoolwork to steer them to feel treasured, accountable, and capable. For example, kids can assist make lecture room decorations, water flora, smooth the board, and do different things inside the study room.

3.5 Join Their Play (And Let Them Lead)

Child-led play includes following your infant's lead. Please help your toddler maintain their interest for a piece on the equal time as longer, which requires retaining a watch on them and responding to what they are announcing and do.

It's realistic to study your toddler's lead due to the truth mastering takes place maximum efficiently whilst a little one is engaged in an hobby. When you play consistent with your child's pastimes, you can use their areas of hobby to interact them in play-primarily based definitely mastering.

Your toddler develops conversation abilties and learns the way to effect the world round them after they take the initiative.

three.6 Focus On Improving Kids' Confidence

Set aside time to location the electronics away, block out thoughts of labor or unique distractions, and make sure that you offer the kid together together with your undivided interest to assist them enjoy valued and confident.

Teachers would possibly in all likelihood make use of the time to interest mostly on their children and pay near interest to what they need. Giving children reward commonly will no longer assist, but giving them positive praise will help them revel in more confident. Parents have to spend healthful time with their kids to show them they're profitable due to the fact that love and elegance are critical factors of self notion and self confidence.

Take him on excursions, proportion meals, play video games, spend time out of doors, or engage in every other hobby a good way to increase the bonding among you and your teen.

3.7 Teach Them How to Set and Achieve Goals

Goal-placing is a capability you can train your infant because it's miles crucial for grit development and generally accomplishing

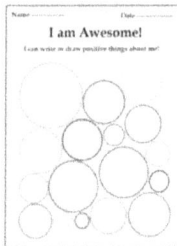

your desires in lifestyles.

Other justifications for schooling aim-setting in your teen are as follows:

It instills duty for his or her actions and training, encourages and motivates their mentality, and creates a robust habit in case you want to last a whole life.

Please help your infant expand ONE essential aim she wants to accomplish this one year.

Make certain the motive is plain, quantifiable, and trackable. Make wonderful the aim may be measured on your baby to look her progress within the course of it.

3.Eight Resist Comparing Them to Others

Children are all unique. They broaden at one in every of a type expenses, have diverse strengths, and feature numerous abilities and pastimes. So put an give up to evaluating your infant to others—a common approach for comparing your infant's usual performance in comparison. Instead, decide whether or not or no longer your infant's academic achievements are "famous," better, or exquisite through evaluating their grades to the ones of diverse university students.

Sometimes the high-quality cause of comparing your little one to others is to foster competition in them, motivating them to achieve success with the useful useful resource of having them execute to the super of their abilities. Performance is maximum genuinely fueled via competition. But it may satisfactory be used wisely, and keeping off this technique of evaluating your children with one among a kind kids is higher.

Ask your little one to fill out the subsequent strengths worksheet to live first-class.

three.Nine Encourage Them to Try New Things to Develop New Skills

Start with little difficulties at the same time as engaging kids to attempt new sports. Daily accomplishments. He'll finally be prepared to address large new demanding situations if he builds self perception with the little things first. Children are more likely to collaborate even as they're able to do the responsibilities they need or desire to complete. Additionally, they may be less inclined to lose their mood and act out. As a give up end result, assisting children in growing new talents can play a extremely good function in behavior control.

Children broaden independence, self warranty, and arrogance as they accumulate new abilities. Therefore, encouraging children's gaining knowledge of can be a critical problem in promoting their whole

Name —————   Date —————
Draw your favorite drawing.

increase.

three.10 Help Them Overcome the Fear of Failure

Children who discover ways to fail and get back up are extra resilient and geared up to address life's challenges. Children who dread failure are much more likely to enjoy tension and tantrums even as mistakes are made. It is difficult, but parents want to try and stand back and allow youngsters room to make errors. They will now not be able to try once more if you continuously watch over their shoulder, schooling them. They require that enjoy to expand and take a look at.

Worry is much more likely to increase in kids who've now not located to truely be given failure. The inevitable failure causes meltdowns, whether or not it takes place in preschool or college. But, extra notably, it'd deter children from trying some thing new or attempting new pursuits.

The following coping worksheet will help child manage their anger.

3.11 Encourage Them to Express Their Feelings

When youngsters can not get you to apprehend how they may be feeling, it makes them more frustrated. So the number one diploma is to assist your teenager in identifying their feelings and the reasons of these emotions. Leading through instance is the super approach to encourage your youngsters to speak their emotions. Start with describing your personal feelings and the extraordinary strategies to talk them.

Please supply your infant the danger to brainstorm solutions for various troubles, after which you may talk whether or no longer or no longer those options are appropriate for the suitable context. Set a first rate instance on your baby through way of modeling effective emotional expression. Use language they're able to recognize and supply an cause for your intentions whenever you operate a word with a enjoy.

3.12 Surround Them with Positive, Confident People

Encourage them to recognize that everyone makes errors and that the maximum important element is to transport on from them. Confident humans do no longer permit their worry of failure hold them all over again, now not because they will be certain they will in no manner fail, but as a substitute because of the truth they may deal with failure gracefully.

Tell your youngster that you'll usually love him. Good grades or terrible grades, be

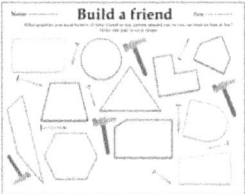

successful or fail the large recreation. Even if you disagree with him, ensuring your infant is aware about how a good deal you price them will lead them to revel in better about themselves, no matter the fact that they lack self-guarantee.

Chapter 4: Problem-Solving Skills for Kids 7-14

Everyone need to treatment everyday problems. But we want to examine the talents we need to do that; they're no longer some issue we are born with.

It is useful that allows you to: pay attention cautiously, count on, check your options, and appreciate the dreams and views of others while addressing troubles.

To gain concessions, negotiate. These are lifestyles competencies which is probably fantastically appeared in both social and professional settings.

Problems are regularly resolved thru speak and negotiation. The first step at the same time as fixing the trouble is identifying the trouble. It could make it plenty much less difficult for anyone to recognize the difficulty uniformly. It's first-class to collect anyone impacted with the useful useful resource of the problem earlier than putting it into phrases that may be solved.

Help your toddler or youngsters pick out out out the problem's root motive and point of starting.

Do your tremendous to concentrate without disputing or arguing. It will provide you with a danger to analyze the real reputation of your toddler. Encourage your teen to maintain the responsibility out of this phase and supply attention to the trouble.

four.1 Problem-Solving Skills Prepare Students for Future Careers

The functionality to collaborate with others is one of the most essential talents college students want to thrive at artwork. To make contributions effectively to initiatives, youngsters ought to discover how to talk, make concessions, and percent credit score score. Encouraging teamwork on precise projects and assignments can be taught in the classroom.

Graduation marks the beginning of actual life for college students in masses of techniques because of the fact that they may eventually placed their education to apply and control their budget and plans. Schools have to address wherein students will pass when they understand the statistics in preference to absolutely inside the occasion that they have. Taking the amazing direction possible and traveling the right path are vital in the workplace. Giving college students context for making options and resolving troubles can help them undergo in thoughts this in immoderate school.

Students can collect those crucial capabilities thru being recommended to self-direct and take obligation for his or her training via independent observe and group paintings. Additionally, selling lateral thinking and independence helps scholars increase their problem-fixing talents.

4.2 Problem-Solving Skills Build Confidence

Kids can gain more self-assurance in choice-making and interpersonal abilties while they might correctly deal with statistics. The way of problem-fixing and choice-making then consists of those developments proper into a continuum. Improved hassle-solving competencies will growth self-self assurance and make you more likely to explain the problem in reality in advance than looking for solutions and plenty a great deal less inclined to transport for a quick restore. With such trouble-solving abilities, kids can fend off the human nature of impatience and enjoy extra comfortable, taking time to provide you with an cheaper answer.

Even if you do no longer assume your kids are natural trouble-solver, you may cause them to attract near the skill. The self warranty they earn will hold to increase over the years as they boom trouble-solving talents to make higher alternatives.

four.Three Go Step-By-Step Through the Problem-Solving Sequence

When you run out of alternatives, the following 6 degrees for hassle-fixing may be beneficial. You can use them to deal with maximum problems, at the side of hard alternatives and interpersonal confrontations.

Your teen is likelier to apply the ones techniques to their problems or disputes with others if you exercise them at domestic.

•The first degree in problem-solving is trouble identity.

•Examine the motives of the trouble.

•Help the child or youngsters choose out the problem's root motive and detail of basis.

•List capability remedies for the problem.

•Make a list of every answer you and your toddler need to provide you with. You are seeking out quite a few alternatives, every reasonable and illogical. Try not to speak about or select the ones but.

•Review the available options for the trouble.

•Consider each answer's blessings and drawbacks in turn.

•Implement the answer.

•Plan out the specifics of the answer while you've got reached an settlement. Then, analyze the outcomes of your trouble-fixing strategies.

•After the kid or children effectively put in force the plan, you need to have a have a look at how it went and help them within the event that they need to copy the machine.

four.Five Define the Problem

Finding the deliver of the issue is the first step in fixing a trouble, as obvious as it could

sound. Unfortunately, locating the muse of the trouble on occasion entails extra research. Ask yourself the five whys within the event of a trouble: Who, What, When, Why, and Where. Then, educate your youngsters to decide an appropriate deliver of the trouble with the useful resource of using questioning themselves the ones questions about it. There are numerous steps children can follow to discover a problem if this is insufficient extra as it must be.

4.6 Encourage creativity

Show enthusiasm with their innovative endeavors. Show a eager hobby in what your youngster famous as a innovative pursuit. Find out for them, for instance, wherein education are supplied or machine can be borrowed, rented, or bought. By constructing costumes or supplying some thing device you can have, provide to assist.

Allow your infant to strive a few diverse subjects. What on the start appearance seems captivating should grow to be being too difficult or unsuited to their person. Also, don't forget that unless the interest is annoying your infant, you have to now not permit them to go away schooling earlier than the give up of a time period. Children have to apprehend that self warranty in a challenge comes from repeated exercising.

Tying creativity in kid's development to a specific artwork form or craft makes no experience. Numerous exciting hobbies foster creativity. For instance, a baby's experience of rhythm, melody, concord, and timing can all be advanced with the aid of approach of creating a song and dancing to song of all genres. In addition, via discussing normal snap shots of natural beauty at the side of your kids, together with the sample on a tree's bark, the shape of a seed pod, or the veins in flower, you could inspire them to be aware records like patterns, shades, shapes, strains, and textures.

Many artwork sports activities also are held for children, specially inside the path of university breaks. Bring them to the park's sports activities, concerts, exhibits, pantomimes, and avenue plays. Talk in your teenager about their responses as you proportion your insights.

When your infant creates their song, theatre, or art piece, make the effort to recognize and applaud their efforts. It is the reason the painting is on the refrigerator. Not as it's lovely however as it suggests our kids that we apprehend their modern endeavors. When imparting comments, try to keep away from being vital. Instead, inspire them to exercise and take specific care of any instruments or device they'll be in fee of.

Above all, don't forget that creativeness and the humanities are as herbal and critical to a toddler's boom as lively exercising, which aids in growing coordination and strength.

four.7 Have Patience

The maximum critical motion in workout tolerance as a determine is listening. Your teen needs to take a look at which you are listening to them and taking them critically. Ask your youngster what is bothering them by stooping to their degree. To show off that you are paying interest, pay them hobby, repeat only some words or terms, and make eye contact. Your teenager is probably extra willing to take note of you if you be privy to them. They will apprehend that you fee and comprehend them.

You can use Patience as a tool in severa events. Most of the time, human beings will no longer come to be irritated once they absolutely choose to keep and understand its blessings. You effects choose it up and use it; you do no longer suddenly discover Patience via tripping over it.

four.Eight Play Problem-Solving Games

A little one's life is enriched through splendid play, which moreover paves the way for them to end up resourceful, lively green human beings at some point of their lives. Likewise, thru incredible play, adults can take a look at, enlarge, invent, clear up issues, research what works and what does no longer, and improve relationships with every distinct.

Game gambling additionally allows in physical growth and motor skills. One of their super features is that interactive video video video games often demand kids to use their arms or our our bodies by a few way. It additionally lets in intellectual growth, reminiscence retention, social competencies, relationships, and friendships.

Use the following commands to resolve if you have any troubles.

4.Nine Ask for Their Help

Kids rely upon their parents, caregivers, and super honest humans of their lives, so extra younger children are expert at soliciting for assist. We regularly introduce independence and self-reliance in children as they mature, but taking some time regarding on line safety is vital.

Asking for assist can be awkward, and some human beings say they must be given their egotism to do it. Reaching out and admitting that you are suffering, are unsure of something, or simply need someone to weep on takes braveness. For younger human beings to achieve lifestyles, they need to learn how to ask for useful useful useful resource.

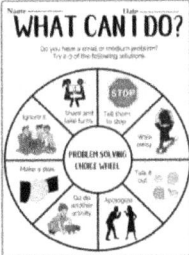

Chapter 5: Improve Kids' Behavior Through Fun Activities

Fostering your infant's social improvement have to have an splendid, lengthy-lasting effect on their existence. People with robust social competencies often have an know-how of at the identical time as to speak, a manner to act in numerous conditions, and a way to make smart choices.

Many kids examine correct social competencies on their non-public thru everyday interactions with the human beings of their lives, on the same time as a few require greater specific social information coaching. There are many interesting approaches to help your youngster growth social capabilities. These pastimes also are notable opportunities for determine-baby relationships.

Whether your toddler is a infant, a preschooler, or has just started kindergarten, socialization sports and video video games are a first-rate technique to learn how to act round their classmates. Playing video games can assist kids have a look at social competencies, emotional manipulate, and body language.

5.1 Notice Good Behaviors

Your little one values your and the alternative caregivers' hobby. Toddlers and preschoolers require a large amount of grownup hobby. Both accurate and terrible hobby is feasible. Give them first-rate praise to expose them they've carried out something.

When you provide kids with suitable, regular recommendation, they fast select out out up appropriate behavior. It includes worthwhile your toddler for particular conduct in vicinity of punishing them when they do some factor you discover objectionable. Your baby frequently appears to you for steering at the manner to behave; what you do subjects a whole lot greater than what you're announcing. Give your baby rewards once they behave in a manner you like.

Name: ————————   Date: ——————
Write about a situation when you did something
awesome. What you feel after doing so.
Will you again do that?

5.2 Handle Stress with Patience

As all dad and mom are aware, coaching children Patience is difficult however essential. In the near term, schooling children patience can assist save you impulsivity and acting out. Our test demonstrates that impatience over the long time predicts quite some eventual problems. It can enhance running relationships, lessen pressure and struggle, and help you achieve your lengthy-term personal and expert goals. Impatience is a hassle for lots humans. Learn to understand the highbrow and emotional signs and symptoms and symptoms that accompany it and the conditions that set it off.

When matters do now not even flow into at the speed that fits our minds, Patience lets in

When I feel stressed

us to control our impulses without troubles. However, the pace of change may probable deliver the affect that issue is shifting speedy. The following worksheet will help to manipulate stress after understanding the pressure emotions.

5.3 Be Consistent with Routines

Family existence runs extra with out problems at the same time as there are each day rituals. Families can spend greater time collectively way to them as well. Children advantage from workouts with the resource of feeling steady, gaining existence abilities, and forming wholesome conduct. Parents who follow

My Daily Schedule

exercises experience extra organized, have much less stress and characteristic extra loose time. According to research, kids, specially extra more youthful youngsters, take a look at from the form of experience of shape. While there are various reasons youngsters want a recurring, in step with parenting specialists, the most vital one is that it offers kids a enjoy of safety.

Kids can make their each day time table as in the following worksheet.

five.Four Communicate with Your Child

Developing a strong relationship among you and your little one is based upon on open communication, making it plenty much less complicated for you to talk approximately hard topics with them as they age. Learning a way to reply to conduct is one of the maximum tough skills to accumulate. Find out extra about strengthening interplay collectively together with your child by means of using using the use of reward, playing, and actively listening. Developing your child's arrogance calls for powerful -way communique. While encouraging and praising your infant will assist them develop, being attentive to them may assist them sense cherished and treasured.

five.Five Keep A Positive and Happy Environment at Home

An enriched and stimulating domestic environment promotes sound boom and

thoughts development by way of giving a toddler affection, emotional assist, and learning and discovery opportunities. Economical and emotional assets are often scarcer in families with first-class one determine. An enriched and stimulating domestic environment promotes sound increase and thoughts improvement through manner of way of giving a infant affection, emotional beneficial aid, and studying and discovery possibilities.

You play a key role in organising a supportive social and emotional climate primarily based mostly on relationships of care and responsiveness for younger kids. Before they revel in stable, children can not find out and studies, revel in themselves, or be in awe. They need to trust of their careers and make certain their dreams might be glad.

A thankfulness worksheet can help enhance gratefulness in kids.

5.6 The Cheer-Up Games

The Cheer-Up Game is exceptional for growing empathy abilities, which can be commonly important. Children regularly find it difficult to understand how others revel in; but, this sport will permit them to image what it can be need to revel in every distinctive man or woman's emotions. Playing this sport with all your kids or possibly their buddies is lots of amusing.

Games frequently name for cooperation, which teaches children to cooperate, take delivery of as authentic with, and paintings as a crew. Interactive video games may additionally additionally moreover help kids enlarge their social skills early on, laying a stable basis for them to gather on

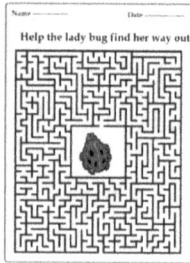

as they mature. Social talents are a vital developmental milestone with a view to advantage your children in the course of their lives.

Kids will revel in solving the following maze.

5.7 The Hot or Cold Game

Select one player to behave because the Hunter and direct them to vacate the location or element techniques with the enterprise.

In the place wherein you play, bury a tiny item or prize.

Re-enter the gambling region with the Hunter, and teach them to move approximately the region looking for the hidden item. When the Hunter is a protracted manner from the reason, say "less warm."

Say "less warm" to the Hunter to permit them to recognize you are moving far from the hidden object. Words that denote diverse ranges of cold, which includes "freezing" or "icy," may be used within the event that they maintain to transport inside the opposite direction.

When the Hunter is close to the intention, say "hotter." Speak the terms "burning" or "warm" as they technique. When the Hunter discovers the object, the sport is over.

Give extra suggestions till the Hunter discovers the concealed object. Play the sport till each participant has had an opportunity to go searching.

Chapter 6: Mental Health Worksheets and Activities for Kids 7-14

Our social development and modern day welfare may be greater by manner of creating an funding time in a interest or hobby. According to research, those taking thing in sports are tons much less possibly to revel in pressure, depressive signs and symptoms, and awful temper. You will experience happier and greater snug after acting sports activities that get you moving spherical.

Kids and younger children can keep brilliant intellectual fitness via keeping bodily fitness, eating a balanced weight loss plan, undertaking common exercise, having the freedom and time to play inside and outside, and being a member of a circle of relatives that commonly gets along. Exercise improves your temper thru freeing molecules like serotonin and endorphins. Additionally, it assist you to depart your house, interact with

Mental Health Matters

others, and reduce emotions of isolation and loneliness.

6.1 Thought Record Worksheet

To discover and modify intricate beliefs, cognitive-behavioral remedy (CBT) makes use of concept recorders as a tool. Keeping a idea magazine will help youngsters develop the dependancy of observing their thoughts and looking for to regulate them. For many conditions, cognitive behavioral remedy consists of the usage of notion recorders. They are useful because of the reality they help us understand the awful computerized mind we've. They assist in recognizing any issues with questioning.

6.2 The Feeling Wheel

A emotions wheel lets in to prevent hiding at the back of the fast or normal solution on the route to being sincere, inclined and practicing dependable life. Increased specificity in expertise and empathizing with feelings results in extra comfort and real honesty. If your infant has been away from you at school, use the wheel at the same time as you communicate to them approximately their day. They speak their emotions finally of the conditions they proportion as they debrief. According to the wheel, as well as the previously recorded occasions, they label their emotions.

Ask the child to fill out the feeling wheel to apprehend the feelings and sports behind that feeling.

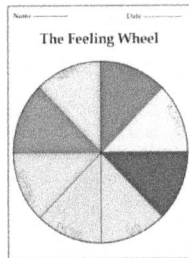

6.Three Daily Mood Tracker

You can higher manage your children's moods and get better extra speedy in case you comprehend them. By turning into more privy to moods, you may higher manage lifestyle selections, decide at the best route of motion for your kid's health, prevent or smash the things that make a kid experience terrible, and searching for to decorate your pleasant of existence.

In addition to creating the teen feel better understood, this permits parents to stay related and beneficial of their toddler's care. Peace and intimacy are brought about with the resource of information one another. Many kids revel in keeping song of things on their telephones, whether or no longer or not via an app or a be aware. Using coloured notebooks or paper for monitoring can be beneficial for folks who revel in creativity.

6.4 Mindfulness Exercises for Children

According to analyze, practising mindfulness can assist kids growth their recognition, awareness, recognition, lecture room engagement, and compassion.

It furthermore enhances

•Academic success, conflict-decision abilties, and famous properly-being.

•Stress, melancholy, tension, and disruptive behavior are reduced.

•Enhanced attention, reputation, and cognitive growth.

•Improved social and emotional talents, along with accelerated empathy.

•Better behavior at university.

•Increased sturdiness.

•Improved control over one's emotions.

•Less pressure and anxiety.

6.Five Mental Health Management Bingo

Mental Health bingo is an exciting undertaking that may be achieved inside the classroom. While it tries to increase attention of the cost of healthy coping mechanisms, it can furthermore be a extraordinary way for college university college students to connect and observe sparkling, powerful strategies of maintaining their intellectual fitness.

Bingo is a activity that every kids and adults experience, and playing it has pretty a few advantages: Playing bingo permits you grow to be greater adept with numbers, which include wide variety popularity. It improves social competencies. It improves intellectual standard overall performance.

6.6 Things I Want to Talk About

The improvement of verbal exchange skills in children starts offevolved offevolved at beginning. Young youngsters can be talked to every time, anywhere, and about the whole lot! By pausing and giving children a hazard to react, you may assist them study communicate—children's language development advantages from analyzing, tune growing a song, and rhyming.

You can ask approximately their favorite person, superpowers they could maximum want to personal, their favored TV program, who they may be grateful to, and masses of others.

6.7 My Feelings

Children can test feelings via feeling charts, so one can help them apprehend, interpret, and explicit their bodily sensations. New neural connections are usual. As a prevent give up result, they may be connecting the advanced analyzing mind to the decrease reactive thoughts.

Children who're better emotionally and intellectually adept and conscious can manage relationships, manage their feelings, and take care of problems when they get up. However, in assessment to many people, it is

able to be difficult for youngsters to discover and realize their very very own and one of a kind people's emotions with out grownup help.

Ask the child to write down down approximately the situations, emotions, and why those happened.

6.Eight Dealings with My Worries

My troubles worksheet is an tremendous tool for helping youngsters confront their issues and fears in a way that feels herbal to them.

On each finger of the concerns worksheet, university college students are informed to put in writing the names of five sincere

people they experience snug discussing their problems. This worry worksheet tries to keep to children that they may be no longer helpless and feature lots of help.

6.9 How can I Improve

Children have to have a pleasant self-image to boom self assurance and resiliency even as encountering new issues. Use this hobby to help youngsters experience higher approximately themselves. You can also additionally moreover provide writing activates that spotlight their unique characteristics.

While describing physical attributes is easy, children can also use phrases like "tough-running," "being concerned," or "a extraordinary buddy" to offer an reason behind their personality. In addition, children can choose to particular themselves visually thru drawings.

6.10 My Motivational Worksheet

In addition to being incredible in and of itself, motivation is a key predictor of mastering and achievement. Students greater pushed to analyze do higher in class and on standardized exams, endure longer, and located up higher-excellent attempt.

Worksheets designed to sell vanity and self warranty in youngsters and teens. Children can apprehend their strengths, growth self-

self notion, and create a extremely good self-image with the help of gear.

Chapter 7: Importance of Mental Health in Kids

Changes and sports from which children typically take a look at, behave, or manage their emotions are highbrow conditions in children. These deviations create distress and make day by day obligations tough. Many children periodically undergo tension, worry, or act out in disruptive techniques. The teen may moreover moreover suspect having a intellectual sickness if their signs and symptoms and signs and symptoms are immoderate, persistent, and intrude with their capability to carry out at play, domestic, or school.

The absence of a highbrow sickness does no longer handiest represent intellectual health. Children with the equal identified intellectual illness may have functions and flaws in how they growth and manage, as well as variations in preferred nice of lifestyles, relying on whether or not or no longer they've got a intellectual contamination. You can Understand how well children are doing through looking at intellectual nicely-being as a scale or through looking for particular thoughts problems.

Understanding Mental Health of Kids

The bodily requirements of a child are smooth for parents to recognize: a healthful diet regime, warmness apparel in bloodless weather, and a suitable bedtime. The toddler's highbrow and emotional desires may not be as apparent.

Children having appropriate intellectual fitness can expect rationally, develop socially, and pick up new talents. You can decorate the development of self-self guarantee, robust vanity, and exquisite emotion in youngsters thru encouragement, character assist, and actual buddies.

WhatIs Mental Health?

Children's mental fitness consists of achieving cognitive and physiological milestones and gaining high high-quality social talents and trouble-fixing strategies. A infant's proper development relies upon in big element on their mental fitness. It aids inside the development of children's remarkable interpersonal, emotional, behavioral, cognitive, and verbal exchange abilties. It additionally builds the concept for reinforcing intellectual health and properly-being later in life.

Children with intellectual health issues can also have problems with their behavior, social interactions, and intellectual and emotional increase. Mental health issues are defined as problems which can be intense, continual, and cause reduced functioning. Promoting precautionary sports activities and remedies can decorate children's properly-being and prevent problems from worsening.

Why Is It Important?

Mentally healthy youngsters revel in happy and assured about themselves maximum of the time. They stay calm and composed in tough situations or even as matters do now not pass as planned. They revel in lifestyles, analyze nicely and assemble strong relationships with own family and friends. They can manage their emotions of sadness, fear, or anger and might recover from problems consequences with out getting depressed. They are continuously open to attempting new or difficult subjects.

The Role of Elders inside the Mental Health of Kids

Every decide's ideal is to offer their kids with law and strong moral thoughts thru amazing parenting techniques. But it isn't a smooth challenge. Additionally, it's far crucial to understand that the figure-little one correlation is a couple of paths and that a parent and their little one are basically in a partnership.

Children's health and protection are ensured with the resource of parents and caregivers, who additionally offer aid to their youngsters to get fulfillment in their coming life and educate them important cultural values. Children gather love, popularity, praise, encouragement, and steering from their mother and father and unique caregivers. They provide the most personal setting for nurturing and safeguarding children as they develop bodily, mentally, emotionally, and socially, in addition to their identities and personas are common.

Mental Health and Social Strength in Kids

The three pillars of circle of relatives lifestyles have to be love, safety, and attractiveness. Children have to apprehend that your affection for them is unconditional and unrelated to their achievements. Failures and mistakes should be expected and stated. Confidence grows in a own family whole of unrestricted love and affection.

Children advantage a preference to look around and understand their surroundings at the same time as their first steps or flair for mastering a latest enterprise is suggested. Allow youngsters to play and discover in a protected location in which they may now not get damage. Ensure them through grinning and interacting with them frequently.

Participate actively of their sports activities sports. Your interest boosts their experience of self confidence and self belief. Young children need to set dreams that align with their aspirations and talents. Do no longer keep your youngsters in the darkish approximately your errors. They need to apprehend that mistakes are some issue all of us make. Knowing that grownups make silly mistakes can be substantially reassuring.

All this guide given with the resource of way of grownups will expand social energy in children, and they will be very a hit in their social participation inside the future.

Chapter 8: Games and Activities to Boost Self-Esteem in Kids

What you think about your self is shallowness. In extraordinary phrases, arrogance is one's truly well worth in their sight. In kids, vanity is vital in their character building and highbrow fitness. Kids having arrogance can perform better of their lives and function wholesome minds and souls. Self-esteem is an indication of authentic intellectual and highbrow health. It allows kids to manipulate all of the problems and annoying conditions of their way.

Kids having low or no conceitedness feels annoyed, involved, and angry. They be bothered via anxiety and depression. Sadness frequently prevails in their moods. They are introverted and do no longer experience social sports activities. Such kids lack coping capabilities and preference powers. They can't undergo the pressures, and their intellectual fitness is commonly now not particular.

Developing conceitedness in kids could be very critical and plays a essential feature in making them glad, confident, and triggered. Self-esteem makes children capable and self-worth. They revel in satisfied for what they may be and expand a healthful thoughts. If you help your children beautify their vanity, they'll be able to overcoming their errors and could not get discouraged thru their screw ups. Kids with vanity can carry out sports activities self-sufficiently and function first rate desire-making capability.

Kids can decorate their intellectual health via arrogance, problem-solving and behavioral development. When you deal with those key factors, their intellectual health may even improve, and they will be able to manage their expressions and emotions.

Self-Esteem Concept

Through shallowness, male children can carry out outstandingly and reap their desires. Self-esteem makes youngsters assured enough to participate and have interaction in healthy sports. It keeps them stimulated and improves their powerful behavior. Self-esteem is the precept simulator to improve social capabilities within the kids and purpose them to cushty at the same time as managing others round them. Kids were confident, remained open to new traumatic conditions, and tried new matters. It will help their mind to growth wholesome.

Make Kids Feel Noble and Appreciated

The major issue you could do for your youngsters is to steer them to enjoy honorable. Appreciate them for his or her efforts. Appreciation will maintain their morale excessive and could purpose them to ardour-pushed. Your children's mental growth depends particularly on the way you solution their efforts. When you recognize your youngsters, they will discover ways to gratitude. Gratitude is a expertise that allows you to make your infant thank complete for what they've got instead of making them complainers.

You have to make your infant feel noble and preferred thru giving them entire interest and remarkable time. Show them unconditional affection via hugs and kisses. Regardless of what comes after an try, try and make your youngsters sense that you accept as true with them and you're with them in their efforts. You can without problems deal with maximum of your children' behavioral troubles with the warmth of your affection.

Foster Their Independence

Focus more on helping your little one in making choices and imparting space for introspection and mistakes in region of carefully monitoring every float they make. Encourage your little one that will help you in home duties like going to the grocery store and helping you pick out out grocery gadgets or a few different low-danger methodologies to foster unbiased alternatives. Give your little one coins to shop for the video video games or garments they need, and allow them to pick out their preferred social sports activities. Having a greater feeling of duty is vital for fostering independence and responsibility.

You can foster independence to your kids with the useful resource of retaining the following subjects in mind;

•The safety of your toddler comes earlier than any yearning for freedom.

•Despite growing little one independence, parental manage is maintained.

•Actively concentrate at the same time as posing inquiries.

•Ask youngsters to make an effort to don't forget or foresee possible outcomes.

Along the manner, your teen have to show signs and symptoms of maturity and obligation. It takes time to end up mature and impartial. For instance, permit your baby be unbiased from taking small options to medium after which to the large selection. Maintain your composure and unique empathy in location of rage. By teaming up with them, you could encourage kids' natural and healthy developmental urges for independence.

Things "I Like About Myself" Worksheet

All human beings are precise and characteristic special trends in them. They behave in a unique manner consistent with their person developments. It is self-esteem that in a role us to assess ourselves. It may be something we don't forget ourselves, like "I am worthless" or possibly "I am nicely really worth ."Boosting arrogance makes us experience truly really worth of ourselves.

We all want to discover the nice traits we've were given in our personalities in great methods. Help your child to apprehend the good person they've got with the useful resource of exploring them. In the subsequent worksheet, the child wants to write down all of the first-rate matters they have got after thinking attentively.

Write A Gratitude Journal or Use Self-Esteem Journaling Prompts

Whether your infant maintains a diary on their private or collectively in conjunction with your assist, journaling may want to have many blessings. Journaling can provide kids a manner to file their thoughts and recollections further to training writing. Journaling furthermore teaches mindfulness, which has the brought benefit of enhancing your infant's temper and highbrow health. Kids can use journaling as a way to research and explore all the feelings which might be brewing interior of them.

It can also be an powerful education tool, encouraging introspection, important questioning, and the development of writing talents. A innovative set off is meant to inspire youngsters to problematic on their mind and drift them inside the proper course. It promotes kid's crucial wondering and the boom of a miles wider worldview.

Practice Positive Affirmations

Children can help themselves with the aid of manner of the use of mantras and powerful affirmations as useful device. They beneficial useful aid in forming an exquisite intellectual, social, and emotional outlook and a strong sense of self-worth.

Children and teens can use a awesome affirmation listing with the resource of using reading the phrases aloud or themselves, discussing how they might help, and deciding which phrases could be most effective.

Positive affirmations are succinct declarations of strength and functionality like "I am succesful" and "I am robust." When affirmations are spoken aloud or silently to oneself time and again, they take at the form of mantras.

Chapter 9: Games and Activities to Boost Problem Solving Capabilities

A critical set of cognitive abilties referred to as hassle-solving abilties are installation in a toddler's first few years of lifestyles. All thru formative years and into maturity, those talents are carried out. Problem-fixing is all about the techniques used to give you a solution.

It is determined that kids typically supply unstructured reactions when they face problems without wondering deeply about the ones issues. It is a natural tool; kids behave due to the reality they lack hassle-fixing abilities. With time and properly introducing children with hassle-solving skills, we're capable of boom their talents to remedy the issues because it should be. There are severa video games, worksheets, mediation, and mindfulness sports activities sports to enhance problem-fixing talents in youngsters.

What Is Problem Solving

Problem-fixing includes defining a hassle, identifying its root cause, figuring out, analyzing, and locating out viable answers, as well as putting the ones answers into movement. Through schooling, strive, and knowledge, trouble-solving abilities may be advanced and advanced. As a quit end result, one may also additionally furthermore ultimately be able to tackling extra complex and tough troubles.

What Are Problem Solving Skills

Every day, kids address severa problems, from issues in the classroom to issues in the sports activities area. However, a small percentage of them own an answer for resolving those issues. Kids who aren't adept at addressing troubles can also do away with tackling them once they upward push up.

Do no longer offer help to remedy your toddler's issues as they arise. Instead, guide them as they undergo the tiers of hassle-fixing. When they require assist, offer path; otherwise, inspire independent hassle-fixing.

You should interfere and provide to assist them brainstorm thoughts if they are suffering to hold springing up with any.

Importance of Problem Solving Skills

Children boom the functionality to suppose with willpower and creativeness to incredible ranges. Still, they must achieve this, particularly as they discover ways to address failure and treatment battle. Additionally, fixing problems is one of the most crucial talents youngsters can look at as it prepares them to cope with greater complicated instructional and social problems as they age.

Studies have showed that children having the self guarantee to stand problems can address each scenario in their destiny lives. Children could have a take a look at problem-solving talents thru way of watching their parents or unique individual caregivers whilst they cope with such conditions.

Problem-Solving Strategies and Steps

Another essential life skills for each parents and youngsters is hassle-solving. Following those five steps will assist parents treatment troubles with their youngsters.

1.Define the hassle first. We need to be smooth about the trouble's nature to recognize and speak it correctly.

2.Compile statistics. To address it, acquire all applicable statistics approximately the hassle, inclusive of its reasons, outcomes, and problems.

three.Come up with functionality solutions. Together, come up with each achievable opportunity.

4.Consider your options in advance than choosing one. Decide on the superior alternative after studying the blessings and drawbacks of each. Set a lessen-off date for taking movement.

5.Assess the solution you positioned for the problem. Think approximately the viable implications of your solution.

Puzzles

A toddler's intellect requires engagement to growth and boom, similar to what all of us does. You might be pleasantly amazed to analyze that puzzles can be one of the best strategies to decorate the highbrow well-being of your youngsters if you are looking for an appropriate method.

Ask your teen to coloration the teddy go through within the following worksheet, because the color is written inside the the front of the sizable variety.

Memory Games

Mental skills like focus, recognition, and hobby, can be greater through using gambling memory video video games. Memory video video games allow for crucial concept, which facilitates children expand traditional observational abilities. Playing memory video video games can decorate seen notion.

Classifying and Grouping Activities

Activities that classify and kind gadgets help children expand numerous wondering competencies and lay the muse for future trouble-fixing. The ability to become aware of traits, correlations, similarities, and differences, further to the seen reminiscence and discernment required to assist youngsters find out approximately type and grouping.

The development of first-rate motor abilties is a few different advantage of carrying sports activities. Many categorizations and sorting

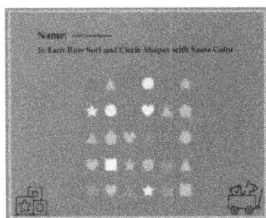

wearing sports are splendid high-quality motor exercising physical sports as properly. In the following worksheet, the child is wanted to type and circle the equal shade shapes in a row.

Building a Maze

Mazes assist children's cognitive talents to enhance. They characteristic in addition to intellectual exercising sports. They are compelled to reason, contemplate, and don't forget on the identical time as tackling the

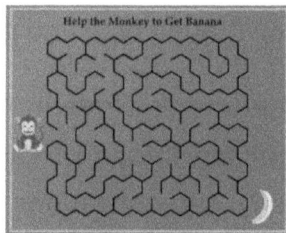

Help the Monkey to Get Banana

troubles. Performing all of these goals together helps human beings's stress tiers, strengthens their consciousness, and hastens their reminiscences.

Find the way for the monkey to get a banana in the following worksheet.

Behavior Charts

A behavior chart is a tremendous technique to encourage your kids with the aid of sharing the ones goals with them and giving them a amusing, visible way to tune their development. You can urge your children to modify their conduct or follow a pattern thru manner of the use of a whole lot of behavior charts and praise schemes.

Tick the column beneath the day you probable did that and circulate even as you likely did not observe the conduct.

Chapter 10: Games and Activities to Improve Kid's Behavior

Your child's boom and welfare want to spend unique time with them. That strengthens your bond, offers your teen more self-self belief, and boosts their behavior.

Consider the sector from your infant's attitude and look at greater approximately their likes, dislikes, troubles, and frustrations. Give your little one your whole attention and convey that they represent the most important key to you. Provide unconditional aid with the useful resource of supplying course, mission communique, and being attentive to them.

Spending time with you may make your infant happier, more comfortable, and increase resilience for adolescence. It is essential to establish the muse early on due to this. While appearing routine responsibilities, you can spend excellent time alongside facet your infant. Alternately, schedule time to play video games, go on walks collectively and do extraordinary activities. Even changing proper recollections together together with your little one can also help enhance your kid's conduct.

Understanding Kid's Behavior

Education and little one care include many elements, which incorporates controlling children's behavior. It is essential to assemble extremely good strategies to help youngsters discover ways to behave effectively. You ought to pay close to interest while kids conflict to find out mind and behaviors.

Life is tough for youngsters or maybe more difficult once they experience by myself. Children experience related and stimulated after they witness adults searching for to understand their perceptions to art work via problems collectively. Understand their emotions, feelings, and expressions to recognize their strengths and weaknesses.

Notice Good Behaviors

Grownups can use the approach of profitable excessive satisfactory actions to recognition greater at the satisfactory behaviors of children in desire to emphasizing their terrible behaviors. Mostly kid's conduct is prompted through the use of the use of what takes location once they precise their feelings. Children's irrelevant behavior often draws adults' be aware.

Primary caregivers' attention is crucial to infants. When you will popularity on appropriate behavior and could forget about some ugly ones, the youngsters will hold up a dependancy of giving them reward. If you deliver youngsters well, common recommendation, they rapid select up suitable conduct. It entails profitable your infant for splendid conduct in place of punishing them when they perform a little aspect you discover objectionable. You want to be beneficial and sincere collectively at the side of your toddler approximately how their movements have an effect on you and may help them understand the way you sense.

Handle Them with Patience

The capability to preserve your composure whilst searching in advance to a preferred or essential very last results is called endurance. Interpersonal patience, existence trouble staying electricity, and each day problems endurance are the 3 primary subtypes of persistence.

Impatience with a teenager traces the bond between you and units a terrible example. When being worried for or being spherical youngsters, it is critical to learn how to allow cross no matter the messes, frustrations, and mistakes a excellent way to always upward thrust up.

You can distance yourself from the state of affairs if you are concerned that your first response might not be taken into consideration one in all patience by means of way of way of taking a step decrease back from it. After doing this, you'll enjoy extra composed and organized to address the imminent conditions.

Spend Quality Time with Them

Spending notable time together with your children will will let you enhance your kid's right conduct and highbrow health. Kids who love to spend time with their families are much more likely to have higher highbrow fitness. Maintaining your children's intellectual and emotional health consists of displaying them your love and hobby.

The pleasant manner to expose your love in your teen is to spend quality time collectively with your children frequently. In popular, spending incredible time with your children is useful for both you and them.

Keep A Positive and Happy Environment at Home

A happy and awesome domestic environment makes kids glad and glad. When we as mother and father carefully attend to our kids's bodily, intellectual, and emotional requirements, their intellectual growth will decorate to the closing mark. Always be available on your kids. Set up your property such that you have easy access to them.

It is crucial in your kid's intellectual fitness to provide them a non violent home environment and to maintain them some distance from home crises. Parents have to additionally make their home smoke-free and from different risky matters for their children' proper bodily and highbrow fitness.

Paly with Sand

Playing dust and soil is a notable manner to enhance motor skills, hand-eye coordination, and muscle power. When your toddler masters the proper shovel grip, they will use their first-class motor talents.

Play with Water

Playing with water is not handiest a a laugh pastime for the kids, however moreover they revel in satisfaction at the same time as playing with water. Lifting, pouring, carrying, sprinting, and splashing assists kids in improving their capabilities in gross motor

flexibility and bodily fitness, even as sports like compressing assist increase the bones in a

little one's palms.

Play with Dough

Your youngsters enhance their little hands as they form play dough into severa shapes. The squeezing, kneading, pulling down, and additional useful resource in developing the hand muscle companies wanted for future tremendous motor abilties like grasping chalk or using scissors.

Drawing and Coloring

Nothing is extra a laugh for youngsters than coloring. It is the maximum satisficing hobby for them. They examine from coloring and endure in mind the colors of things when they do it through themself.

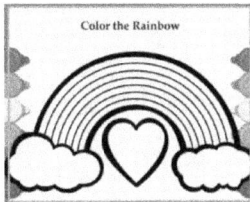

Color the Rainbow

Running, Jumping, Climbing, Swinging

Running, jumping, hiking, and swinging are the video video games youngsters not superb experience however moreover examine new competencies. Playing with pals allows them take a look at social abilties like sharing, being involved, and supporting others.

Chapter 11: Mindfulness and Mental Health Growth

Research demonstrates that mindfulness can help cope with the signs of some intellectual distress and decrease pressure and anxiety. Mindfulness allows children to have a look at with the aid of way of manner of that specialize in what's taking location inside the present 2nd with an expression of friendliness and nonjudgment.

By practicing mindfulness in numerous contexts, along side each formal and casual meditation, youngsters can advantage a clearer mind-set on their lives and create space to endure in thoughts issues from several angles with out becoming pissed off thru tough emotions or mind that would make them sense worse.

What Is Mindfulness and Why It Is Important?

Children and teenagers can rent numerous brief and easy mindfulness strategies even as feeling compelled or traumatic, which incorporates all through test season at college

111

or through an emotionally attempting time. Being aware can actively help the increase of presidency function and cognitive and performance competencies. It can help beginners attention better, pay greater interest, assume more creatively, follow their present day understanding more successfully, enhance running memory, and extend their making plans, reasoning, and problem-fixing competencies.

Mindfulness Tips for Children

Knowing that pressure is a barrier to studying, increasingly more faculties are focusing at the emotional nicely-being in their college students through responsibilities like mindfulness practices, meditation, and the deliver of intellectual health first aiders and pals.

Focusing at the triumphing and keeping a non-judgmental consciousness of internal and outside occasions are key additives of mindfulness. It includes taking note of the frame's bodily and emotional responses, relationships with other people, and the environment.

Preschoolers can gain masses from growing the ones focusing and noticing talents in diverse strategies. Their functionality for sustained recognition is improved. It aids in pressure control and operational nicely-being.

Mindfulness helps people come to be more emotionally clever and on pinnacle of things of their reactions. They gain from having a more hobby in their senses and our bodies. It enables the development of a dating with nature. Kids get facts and kindness for others as a stop result.

The Role of Mindfulness On Mental Health

Kids do no longer want to depart the whole lot at the back of to practice mindfulness. Mindfulness can do magic at the identical time because the mind is busy anywhere else and the body some place else. With exercise, kids can get their minds centered at the triumphing second. It is a completely useful approach to acquire a peaceful thoughts with a brilliant mindset.

Although the blessings of mindfulness and meditation were noted for masses of years, neuroscientists have located proof suggesting that they preserve youngsters' brains from miserable depend away. It allows boom a brilliant wondering device, growing the regions of the mind worried in getting to know, reasoning, emotional manipulate, empathy, compassion, and attitude-taking. It additionally facilitates reduce worry, tension, and pressure, enhancing interest, focus, and reminiscence.

Mindfulness Breathing

Children can workout respiratory bodily activities to assist them at any time of the day, no matter whether they're feeling disturbing or pressured, want to unwind or doze off, want to calm their our our bodies after an excessive workout, or even simply need to take a harm and regroup even as they're overly energetic.

Mindfulness Breathing

Meditation

Meditation can assist decorate children' sleep, and they awaken with a fresh mind. It enables youngsters growth their recognition and reduce their stress and tension. Meditation moreover makes kids mentally

Color the Sheet & Practice Bubble Blowing for Mindfulness Breathing

strong and self-regulated.

Mindfulness Eating, Walking, and Listening

Practicing mindfulness while consuming, strolling, and listening will boom kids' interest and gaining knowledge of capabilities. They can examine deeply about the taste, sound, and environment.

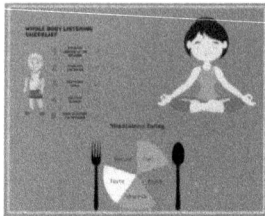

Chapter 12: What is Emotional Intelligence?

Emotional intelligence is loosely described as an ability to recognize, adjust, and manage feelings, your very private and people of diverse people. It modified into generally perception that emotional intelligence changed into, like highbrow intelligence, innate, and could not be found or taught, despite the fact that it is able to be evolved. But emotional intelligence is first-rate a flip of phrase, and need to be treated that way. It should truely as with out trouble be emotional awareness, and focus can in truth be determined and superior; it desires to be for a nicely-advanced man or woman and a properly-functioning network and society.

A man or woman who has mastered emotional intelligence well-knownshows the ones dispositions:

•Awareness of the roots and reasons in their personal emotional impulses

•Awareness of the reason conditions related to which emotional impulses

•Willingness to regulate reason activities associated with emotional impulses

•Willingness to analyze extra approximately the roots, reasons, triggers, and in addition changes

•Awareness of the roots and motives of others' emotional impulses

•Awareness of the reason events related to others' emotional impulses

•Willingness to modify motive situations associated with others' emotional impulses

•Willingness to investigate greater approximately the roots, causes, triggers, and similarly changes of others' emotional impulses

•Willingness to engage in active listening

Note that emotional intelligence isn't pretty a good deal facts these gadgets, but being inclined to alternate one's conduct according with that statistics. If a person is aware about that what they will be doing is delinquent or awful or unsound, however does no longer take steps to exchange their behavior, that is considered disordered behavior. There are volumes on personality issues, however another time, that's not the number one consciousness of this ebook. However, we without a doubt can say that incredibly advanced emotional intelligence, predicated on a sturdy enjoy of empathy and evolved early in life, will lessen the threat of everyone developing harmful person issues later in life. It's additionally noteworthy that some of personality issues begin to enlarge within the teenage and pre-teenage years, so instilling emotional intelligence early on is pretty advocated to set up a healthful psyche. That's now not to mention it can't be superior later in lifestyles if crucial.

Active Listening

A second is needed proper right here to talk approximately the idea of energetic listening. In short, active listening consists of, nicely, actively listening. Active listening consists of:

•Paying interest

•Focusing at the opportunity individual, no longer on yourself

•Ridding your thoughts of distraction

•Not interrupting

•Processing facts

•Imprinting information the usage of repetition and paraphrasing

•Using information to formulate exclusive related summations

•Using records to trouble-clear up

Basically, energetic listening manner you're now not without a doubt sitting there, nodding and smiling and thinking about your subsequent quip. It approach you're paying attention, which you're actively worried with what the other person is saying.

Active listening is paramount to real communications talents, control skills, social competencies, and of course, emotional intelligence. Emotional intelligence is prepared records and dealing with the feelings of others (in addition to your very very own). But how better to apprehend what inspires the feelings of others round you than to pay interest after they percent approximately themselves? You'll need to solicit that information, and also you'll actually need to endure in mind it. That will assist you grow to be aware of and avoid their triggers, despite the fact that they may be capable of't achieve this themselves. But, of course, if we're talking about children, they may possibly not percentage an grownup's excessive emotional intelligence!

Active listening manner you care; it approach you're no longer constantly wondering handiest of yourself. It technique you have got empathy, and that is crucial to emotional intelligence, further to such a lot of specific crucial expertise units.

Why is Emotional Intelligence Important?

Some of the blessings of emotional intelligence encompass:

•Less strain

•Increased self-admire

•Better fitness

•Wider social circles

•Wider expert circles

•Greater success

The emotionally clever are not wrestling with their very very own feelings. They not often have emotional conflicts with others, and they make and maintain friends. They provoke those in a feature to offer them possibilities. They have dynamic social and romantic lives. The strength of emotional intelligence in romance is off the charts, however that's now not pretty our recognition right right here! Again, volumes were written, and that may be a ebook approximately circle of relatives.

Conversely, people who lack emotional intelligence are cited for:

•Social isolation

•Depression

•Low self-recognize

•Poor weight loss plan and health

•Stymied social lives

•Stymied expert possibilities

Those who lack emotional intelligence can be emotionally erratic themselves and characteristic contentious relationships with others. This may frustrate them socially, that might hobble someone's personal development with self-medicinal drug, negative eating regimen, reduced conceitedness, expert failure, depression, and an entire host of various troubles.

Having a mastery of emotional intelligence, or lacking one, can ship a person on a trajectory for lifetime happiness or distress. Of route, the man or woman with emotional intelligence will at the least recognize why, on the equal time as the alternative may additionally in no manner benefit any perception.

Awareness.

Mindfulness

When we recollect focus, we're sincerely talking about mindfulness, this is vital to emotional intelligence. It's approximately being measured in our perceptions and our conduct. This whole book is primarily based at the perception that emotional intelligence may be determined and superior, as those are the goals of the e-book: to help you expand emotional intelligence for your youngsters, in yourselves, and to create stronger circle of relatives bonds. You'll moreover have a few a laugh, and who doesn't need that with the circle of relatives?

Mindfulness can follow to a number of behaviors, along aspect:

•Physical warning

•Politeness

•Appreciation

•Communal resource

•Lack of bodily aggression

•Deliberate use of motive

•Empathy

You'll be aware the commonality of these tendencies: All consist of interaction with any other man or woman (or element in a few times). A individual who is aware is aware about every other person's emotions while they're polite and supportive. They are aware of the importance of purpose over emotion and control their very personal physical aggression. They can be cautious of volatile elements like delinquent conduct, which also requires an energetic recognition of diverse people. The whole of our society, of any society, relies on a few manner of reputation of the rights of others and the reasons for those rights.

Empathy can be loosely described as a sensitivity to the feelings of others. It allows us to sense what others enjoy, and that helps us to apprehend one-of-a-type perspectives. That is crucial to emotional intelligence, which incorporates information the emotions of others. Emotions are generated via using human beings, and that they display lots about the ones people (for social purposes, an excessive amount of). So, to understand human beings and address them correctly, one has to have empathy. And empathy is like mindfulness to the max!

Can Emotional Intelligence Be Taught?

Like the whole concept of emotional intelligence, there may be a question as to whether or now not or no longer or now not empathy can be taught. There are volumes approximately the person versus nurture argument and the way it applies to psychology, and this ebook isn't approximately that type of in-depth have a observe. So, as promised, we'll be brief.

Most topics are a combination of nature and nurture.

Boom, problem solved.

True, some human beings have a manifestly more potent revel in of empathy, a few do now not. There are traits of temperament which range from person to individual. Just as human beings are all distinct, there are also variations in cultures. But the ones humans percent not unusual influences, every in a shared household, community, or u.S.A. Of the usa. External sports (nurture) intensify internal strengths or weaknesses (nature) and those matters boom because of this. The internal quickly impacts the out of doors, which impacts the internal in a cycle of nature and nurture. It's now not good enough to excuse maximum behaviors in either kids or adults. That's honestly the way we are, isn't ideal.

The Cycle of Behavior

As prolonged as we're searching at the internal, this is something that everyone who seeks to comprehend emotional intelligence ought to apprehend. There is a 3-step cycle of conduct in humans. If all 3 steps are present and really superior, that man or woman's conduct might be to be ordered. If they may be within the wrong order, or some are skipped, and this is the case in the considerable majority of human beings, that conduct can be disordered. The behavioral cycle is:

•Emotion

•Thought

•Action

After any outside stimulus, the first actual issue that takes area inside the psyche is emotion. This is the number one response in animals, in mammals specifically. Whether it's miles lust, fear, anger, or glee, emotion is the number one thing that takes place.

Thought follows speedy. Emotions are blended with reminiscences and center values. This effects in a decision of movement. People not often act with out wondering, even though best for a cut up-2nd.

The problem is that a break up-second isn't enough for emotion or concept or motion. People aren't planned approximately this cycle, and it results in antisocial conduct. It additionally prevents emotional intelligence. A individual who from time to time feels and great thinks may also additionally moreover act in a way this is cold and missing in trouble for others. A person who feels (a egocentric method commonly) and does no longer remember others earlier than acting is also showing disordered, antisocial conduct. A individual who thinks, then acts, and then feels afterwards is likewise getting it wrong. It's a clean issue to apprehend but an easy element to overlook.

Emotion and Reason

An important observe approximately the cycle of behavior defined above is that it talents feelings (feeling) and cause (belief). These two paintings collectively in a shape of duality we regularly see (think about the Ying and the Yang). Every human psyche has feelings (emotions) and thoughts (purpose). Both are vital to a nicely-adjusted psyche. They regularly impact every other to 3 degree, in advance than motion takes area. Social actions give up result from a balance of emotions and cause, and antisocial moves end result from an imbalance of emotions and motive.

But it's miles essential to remember that one might be superb over the alternative. It isn't unusual and it is contagious that humans act primarily based on their feelings, putting purpose apart. But whilst appearing and behaving in a social region (any interaction among or more human beings), cause want to continuously be successful. Balance is positioned upon mirrored picture, and upon reflected image it's miles purpose which prevails. It is the person of emotion to get up first, but to bypass. Reason stays ordinary, based on statistics which is probably robust even as decrease lower back to for similarly scrutiny. So even as humans act fast (in fact, simply reacting), they will be performing out of emotion. When they respond in time, they will be generally appearing with cause as their fundamental attention, no longer emotion. And even as you or in fact definitely each person is interacting socially, motive want to constantly prevail. The cannot achieve success at the identical time in the equal human psyche. We'll see how all this figures into making the lives of you and your family higher. But for now, preserve those gadgets in mind.

Emotional Intelligence in Children and Adults

Since that could be a ebook approximately families, and is largely a collection of video games for families to increase emotional intelligence (in addition to to reinforce familial bonds), allow's take a short test the man or woman of EI because it applies to adults and to children.

The tenets of each are the equal. But the manifestations of these behaviors range. How do you understand in case your child lacks emotional intelligence? How do you apprehend in case you do? Wait, you aren't the child, are you? If you're, fantastic for you for analyzing this ebook! Whoever you are, the statistics are the same. But youngsters aren't adults, and they may manifestly lack emotional intelligence to a extra diploma. It will change their conduct specially techniques.

Lack of emotional intelligence in every adults and youngsters manifests as:

- Depression

- Aggression

- Regression

But depression is more difficult to discover in youngsters, who can't express themselves. Parents regularly take this for temperament, like shyness. It expresses itself in character or childlike leisure abuses which can be tragically comparable (tablets and alcohol for each) or substantially particular (video video video games and social media, darkish psychology for adults). Regression is much less complex to become aware of in kids, whose development is less difficult to chart and springs in incredible stages, while it does no longer in adults. But adults do this too, the notorious midlife disaster being the maximum instance. Aggression is a good deal much less difficult to discover in every adults and youngsters, but passive aggression is greater not unusual in adults than children, the latter more frequently expressing unfettered aggression.

If any of this sounds acquainted, there might be a loss of emotional intelligence somewhere in your home. And allow's face it, even the ones who have a few emotional intelligence can constantly use a track-up. Mindfulness is planned, however this stuff can also slip with time and inattention.

Well, that's pretty tons all you want to recognize. There's more to it, of path. But if you and your circle of relatives have mastered the whole thing in this economic break, type of 2,000 terms, you will be a beacon of properly-adjusted behavior for the whole neighborhood. But thinking about you acquire this ebook, you could probable already isolate some problem styles growing, for your youngsters or in yourself. And, as we mentioned inner the advent, you're seeking out a way to beautify the ones items on your circle of relatives. You're trying to do it in a way which brings your family together.

Well, we've were given what you've come for. So now which you have a sturdy understanding of what we're all doing, allow's get to art work … or play, because the case can be. Mutual take transport of as actual with, empathy, social interplay, developing own family bonds: These are the foci of the video video games that take a look at.

PART TWO

Emotional Intelligence Games For Your Whole Family

Chapter 13: Games for Young Kids (Ages 4-7)

It's critical to be conscious that the very young can't be predicted to have plenty emotional intelligence. In the primary few years, human youngsters are almost all emotion. Kids don't certainly grow to be what we recall as being self-conscious till they're about four or 5, so this is the age to begin making them aware of their feelings, what brings them on and a way to manipulate them.

But as regards the cycle of conduct, kids earlier than four are all emotion and motion, no notion to each one. Here is in which idea begins offevolved and ought to be nurtured, however assume lots greater reliance upon emotion than perception in advance than movement for kids of this age.

These video games are going to rely extra on talking and plenty tons less on writing, as this is a capacity many young kids are although growing.

INDOORS

The Bye-Bye Game:

This is awesome for youngsters who might also moreover furthermore have separation anxiety, or are displaying signs of it. It's a completely not unusual problem at early a while, specifically for great kids. But for the reason that separation anxiety is certainly the dominance of emotion over motive, it's an early crimson flag of a loss of or want for more emotional intelligence.

Play in any room of the house. Suggest that you play The Bye-Bye Game (say it this way so your toddler can be assured and terrific stepping into). Sit them down and inform them you're going to exit for a second. Tell them that, within the event that they bypass over you, to shout out the silliest word they might think about. This teaches them, in a fun way, to companion emotions with terms and to learn how to express their emotions with phrases (thoughts) earlier than setting them into motion (crying, likely).

On the primary round, step out of the room, but earlier than you close the door, go back and shout out a few crazy word of your own choice. Hug and kiss and reassure your little one. This demonstrates that leaving also can have a tremendous give up give up result, a loving pass back.

Try it again, however this time close the door and live out of the room for, say, five seconds. Whether they call out their non-public phrase or not, pass returned and say your very personal goofy phrase. Then hug and reassure. If they ask why you didn't wait, tell them which you overlooked them. That reassures them that their feelings are mutual and herbal and now not whatever to be fearful of. Extend the period of your absence longer and longer as the game calls for.

As your toddler matures, turn this into a undertaking of cowl and are looking for for, in order to have even more effects on their revel in of hobby, engagement, and playful amusing with their dad and mom. That will resonate with them later, and with you.

Huggy Jail:

Here's a amusing model of a conventional monster chase endeavor, but not as scary for greater younger children. Proclaim that the Huggy Thief (the kid) is on the run, then chase them down. The punishment, of direction, is a brief stay in Huggy Jail, in that you hug and kiss them. This encourages them to run unfastened in preference to being clingy, which is an indication of emotional unintelligence, if you'll. It moreover demonstrates which you are there to appearance out for them, and that no longer all ramifications are terrible. This will help with their capability to stand traumatic situations later in existence.

To keep this game active, and to allow it to hold up alongside aspect your maturing kids, permit them to reveal round and chase you and located you in Huggy Jail. It's as plenty a laugh for you as it's far for them.

Making Faces:

Here's a first-rate exercising to play along with your younger children. This is a incredible way to play on their strengths and to excite each their imaginations and their communications talents. If you've got have been given more than one toddler, it's one you all can play together, so no one has to look ahead to their flip, another factor tailor-made to young youngsters.

Simply acquire their interest (that you'll do at the begin of each undertaking). To start, pick out out out an emotion, and function all and sundry make a face which fantastic exemplifies that emotion. You will participate and lead with the resource of example (as in all of those video games for more youthful children). And allow your example be exaggerated and comical, as a whole lot as you may. And you can! You've been making funny faces at your children for a while, but now you're doing it with a motive. The more they enact the facial talents, the extra they will experience that emotion. Feel free to have all and sundry use their fingers and posture, despite the fact that have them live seated for this exercise.

This recreation, like maximum, is meant to illicit fun and entertainment at a few level in the machine of mastering. So don't pull away from laughing and playing it. When have end up the final time you and your own family sat round with each different giggling?

Popular emotions for this activity consist of:

•Happiness

•Sadness

•Anger

•Surprise

•Shyness

•Confusion

•Curiosity

•Frustration

Take word of your children's reactions. Are they gradual to answer, are they grandly theatrical? Do they chuckle with others, their siblings, or at them? Are they collectively supportive?

Take a higher appearance. When they illustrate frustration or anger or perhaps pleasure, do they direct that at every specific? Does one sibling pay attention anger and turn to their greater youthful or older sibling? When they pay hobby pleasure, which decide do they examine or enact within the route of? We're now not in search of to create rivalries among dad and mom, of route. But if you've ever concerned that perhaps you're no longer connecting as carefully with one infant, this may be revealing. Along those lines, who're you enacting inside the path of for anger or joy or suspicion? Your partner? Your little one? Which one?

This clean game will become an exemplary workout in emotional intelligence, which is largely concerned with know-how how your personal emotions engage in a social context. Who conjures up which feelings in you? That's a purpose element, and some issue you'll should check and adapt to if you're to be properly-adjusted and emotionally practical.

Naming Faces:

Here's a smooth restore and a clean increase on the preceding pastime. This time, pass round from man or woman to individual, each of whom will enact an emotion and others wager which emotion this is. Since your kids won't be of age to be analyzing and writing without difficulty, enjoy unfastened to let them pick out out one off the top in their heads. Use the same feelings you've used in advance than. As the game chief, enjoy loose to whisper a few recommendations proper into a toddler's ear if they might't keep in mind one. This cheat works superb if there

are greater than honestly the two of you!

You can modify the policies if you have children and also you need to have one act and the other guess, and you could useful useful resource each participant within the occasion that they're too extra youthful to improvise and you want to keep subjects sincere.

Making Faces And Bodies:

In the identical way you made faces to present an reason behind emotions, strive it this time in a place in which you've were given a piece greater room. You can play Making Faces over the dinner desk, in case you preference. This time, move into the living room or own family room and make yourselves comfortable. Pick an emotion and, as the game chief, act the emotion out. You can use your face, but rely on your body, your body language. Do no longer communicate inside the course of this sport if you are enacting the emotion, however the guessers can name out their guesses at will. What moves supply frustration, perhaps (pantomiming) pulling out your hair. What moves deliver sorrow or delight? Don't keep over again. And make certain to announce your emotion on the prevent so your extra more youthful children understand the complete connection amongst your expression, that emotion, and the word related to that emotion.

Emotions Charades:

Here we stock the preceding game one step similarly. Pick an emotion and enact it, and instead of pronouncing it, permit the observers call out their guesses. This is a extraordinary recreation for pre-young adults as nicely. As with each model of Charades, no phrases are allowed from the character performing out the riddle.

The Hokey Pokey, Emotional Edition:

This is a first rate sport for more youthful youngsters for such a lot of reasons. It's one of the few singalong video video games we've got, and children love that. It's participatory, and kids love that. And they already understand the track and how it works, and kids love that too.

So begin this model the manner you may give up the equal vintage version, which normally goes from ft to go after which entire self. This time, start with the top, then do the entire self. This is for severa very unique reasons. For sensible features, there's now not enough time and juvenile hobby to artwork your way up the whole frame; that's a unique model of the identical track. You're setting up that the primary deliver is the top (which it is for each emotions and mind, as we recognize). Next, your whole self establishes that the whole thing on your body is suffering from everything to your head. The topics are immediately linked, however the head is number one.

These familiar contributions to the song push us right to the coronary heart of the subsequent verses, if you can.

Next, in vicinity of placing your leg or arm in, you positioned your emotion in. Physically this indicates leaning in advance sincerely a chunk and performing out the emotion in as trustworthy a manner as feasible (so kids can studies them with out problem and speedy). Try these:

•Sad: Flexing your fists in front of your eyes to suggest crying

•Happy: Wide smiles and opened eyes, jazz hands

•Tired: Slouching posture (this is a incredible alternative for melancholy for children of this age)

You also can replacement feelings for behaviors, as the relationship among the ones is crucial to installation in a infant's thoughts:

•Mean: A snarl

•Sweet: Batting your eyes

•Fun: A silly face

•Grouchy: Crossing your fingers inside the the front of your chest

•Silly: Stick your tongue out, make a goofy face (a la Harpo Marx)

This interest teaches kids that emotions are simply as an awful lot part of them as their hands or legs, that they're simply as essential. And really due to the truth the traditional model of the music teaches youngsters to perceive (hands, legs) and organisation (left, right) the usage of factors in their frame, the new edition teaches them the identical problem, to come to be aware of (mad, candy) and employer (emotions, developments). It moreover combines the factors of Making Faces right proper into a track-and-dance layout which more youthful kids can once in a while withstand.

Coloring Emotions:

Kids love coloring, so right right here's a notable manner to appeal to their experience of creative expression. It can also moreover want to cause them to all way of fruitful endeavors and mindfulness later in existence. We'll be coming lower lower returned to this concept in later video video video games, and you'll observe we regularly pass again to ideas we visit in those video games for extra younger kids. In reality, as your children grow to be older, you'll probably be coming another time to the ones principles and this ebook to hold this way of life alive and growing them as your circle of relatives matures.

This time, spread out a few coloured markers (or crayons if you pick) and paper. Acquaint your children with the regulations and motive, like this:

"You realize the manner to shade images of puppies or timber or homes. Now, we're going to shade feelings. Now, permit's remember an emotion. Let's pick out joy. What color does satisfaction experience like, what does it appear to be?"

Observe their alternatives. They'll probable think about it, and don't be amazed to find out girls choosing crimson. They're more or lots much less programmed to do this, however others will though choose out purple or crimson. Red doesn't constantly advocate anger. That in itself is a case-in-point about emotional intelligence. Emotions are complex and they'll be particular to the ones who have them. Each ought to be taken in context and with complete attention for the person. A man or woman is not the equal of their feelings, no longer even in their movements. Emotions and moves are fleeting topics; people evolve through the years, and an entire life is a long term.

Watch in case your children use black to depict pleasure, and puzzle over that conundrum! This exercise will mirror masses approximately a infant's right emotions and perceptions on this way. Interpretation can be a whole lot of fun and may reason terrific conversations that, yet again, will permit you to join emotionally. Don't worry about usually reading plenty into some topics: Why did they pick out out black? Should you be worried? Maybe your infant is definitely in reality into Batman right now!

And don't neglect to have a examine your private picks. What sunglasses recommend joy to you? Why? What establishments do you're making with that shade such that it method joy to you? Understanding those gadgets, even asking yourself the question, will create a bond amongst concept and emotion which we have were given already visible is important to a nicely-balanced psyche.

Now begin coloring. Don't worry approximately shapes. Let the children' instincts, and your very very own, determine what shapes. Perhaps you're shading it in like a sky, otherwise you're making circles or determine eights. Just draw. It's an exceptional concept to have some music inside the records for this sport, but not some factor too distracting. Just enough to offer a few rhythm and innovative belief, even subconsciously.

While coloring, ask your youngsters (one after the alternative) why they selected the shade they determined on, what institutions they have got with that colour. If they don't recognize, that's fine too. The idea is to create the association of concept and emotion.

Pick any other coloration/emotion and keep drawing that emotion, at the same internet web web page because the opportunity. You can coloration in a unique place, or right on top of the previous contribution. Use a few different sheet of paper if you want.

At the prevent, check the outcomes. They will probably be very precis. Use the occasion to see what pix you and your circle of relatives can see in the ones summary shapes and hues. This excites the creativeness and continues the bond of idea and emotion. You may additionally additionally additionally additionally be discovering hidden abilties, or nurturing abilities you comprehend are there. This precept of interpretation is one we'll come lower again to, like extraordinary thoughts we talk in the ones early-age video video games.

Picture This, Jr. Edition:

Before playing this recreation, pop over to the net and print up a few pics. It is flawlessly nice

to print them in black and white. Just search for unfastened images the usage of key phrases of the numerous feelings you're turning into acquainted with using. Make fine frustration or anger are some of the feelings, however don't wonderful encompass negative emotions. Print one for every emotion. Write the emotion in the lower back of the photo, however in pencil and small and positioned wherein best you could see it.

To play the sport, take a seat down with the pix face down in the front of you. Raise one image and characteristic your children guess what emotion they're seeing. Note that they may now not get it proper, and that's true. For one toddler, frustration and anger can also additionally look pretty the same. This may be pretty telling. If frustration and anger are synonymous to your toddler, they're probable to answer to their frustration with anger (or unhappiness with love), and that's what emotional intelligence is meant to reduce down (among diverse things). But frustrated anger is a key signal of a loss of emotional intelligence (as is, of direction, mistaking disappointment and love).

Ask your children to plumb their emotions right right here. Why do they mistake one emotion for some other, in the event that they do? What indicates one emotion over a few other? Ask them to verbalize their feelings of these feelings, some thing they will be. These solutions is probably extra sophisticated as we skip directly to greater tough versions supposed for older children, but that is a golden opportunity to top your children to pursue the relationship among motive and emotion, between reason and effect, and to undergo in mind of various human beings and why they enjoy as they do.

You received't be giving any solutions in this sport, so you're off the hook. But don't be afraid to assignment yourself at the same time as listening to your children's solutions. Do you sympathize with their attitude? What's causing it? Is there a few tremendous way you can affect them based mostly on their answers, possibly a problem stemming out of your private thoughts-set?

Toy With Me:

Here's a version on Picture This, and it builds on those abilities. This one is right to play with one toddler, however it's correct for 2 or three (huge numbers get hard with this endeavor). This one's first-rate for the room in which children often play and wherein their toys are most-frequently saved.

Simply ask your toddler to introduce you to some of their toys, or to speak about them if you're already familiar (you take into account Buzz Lightyear). So, take the toy in question and ask your toddler what emotion they companion with the toy. Is this a satisfied toy, an irritated toy? They're now not all happy anyhow. Darth Vader isn't a totally satisfied chap, nor are one or extra of the Transformers characters, nor might be any array of crammed animals.

Ask your infant to offer an reason of why the characters enjoy as they do. The cause this is such a fun exercise is that the children already recognize the answers; they understand the backstory of Boba Fett or Yoda or a few factor man or woman the toy represents. It's some issue they already have an hobby in, and it performs to their strengths.

It additionally allows them apprehend (through way of verbalizing) the connection among emotion and purpose. Darth Vader is indignant because of the reality his cherished partner modified into misplaced years in advance than. Godzilla is irritated that he modified into awakened from his close eye (which may account for his radioactive breath). One toy or each different can also moreover have a backstory which your little one has created. They also can moreover truely make one up proper away! That's great, it way the game is exciting their experience of narrative, that they're geared up to apprehend some distinct person's mindset and its institutions to their emotions. That is how they'll come to appearance the relationship among their very personal feelings and the things which delivered on them.

Something to take a look at approximately most stuffed animals is that, as frequently as they're well-known characters like Kermit the Frog, they will be regularly greater time-venerated. This offers youngsters the threat to create their private narratives, likely recommended through narratives they recognize or narratives they're residing or take delivery of as proper with they're dwelling. Show interest approximately the crammed animals which don't have regular backstories and ask your children about them. Listen carefully to their solutions, as they may just as results be portray a self-portrait with out information it.

The Ape Family:

Here's a fun exercise for interior or out, a large own family or small. It's a playacting exercise, that you've already finished together together with your circle of relatives with Making Faces. But this one uses the entire frame, and belongs in a larger room like a dwelling room or own

family room, now not the ingesting desk wherein a number of those video video games can sometimes be played.

To play The Ape Family, designate roles inside the family. You may be the parent of both gender, or you may choose out to play a little one and allow a baby play the adult. Many people expect the equal roles in the Ape Family as they occupy in their very own. That's excellent, it's now not the essential trouble.

Now skip about an afternoon in the existence of a everyday human own family. Do cleansing chores, homework, and feature dinner. The rules are, of path, that you can't use any phrases. You can simplest emote so one can get your factors throughout.

It's more hard than you agree with you studied!

You could in all likelihood discover your self getting aggravated, feelings constructing. Who is aware of how topics will flip out? Probably, you'll must calm subjects down, so maintain a watch fixed on it. Of course, whenever feelings be successful and there can be a remarkable lack of purpose, as matters are inside the Ape Family family, things want to be cautiously monitored.

That's the aspect.

Now, we're not seeking to inspire a row alongside aspect your circle of relatives. There's lots to be observed out proper here approximately the manner to examine people, a manner to sympathize with emotional expressions, a manner to better manage your very private frustrations and tendencies to outburst. Parents regularly lose track of that, and an outburst of mood can be very dangerous to youngsters. They also are typically not noted and generally emulated and repeated from one generation to the subsequent.

Outdoors

Stop And Toss:

Here's an wonderful workout for the outdoor, and we don't advocate it for the dinner table or residing room. One test the sport's name will probable inform you everything you need to apprehend approximately why!

This recreation works with numerous kids or possibly surely one! It's right for constructing cooperation amongst siblings or amongst mother and father and children too.

Take the own family out to the outdoor in conjunction with your ball to toss. Establish a rotation, starting with you as the sport leader. As the holder of ball, you could pick out out whom to throw it to, at the side of your self. Passing it to your self way tossing it right away up, no longer a ways, and catching it yet again. But you have got got to name that individual (or yourself) out first. Everybody gets one desire, so in case you choose your self, the ball robotically goes to the following individual within the rotation once you've completed that skip to yourself. If you call out a person across from you and that they pick out out themselves, they throw to themselves after receiving the ball from you, after which of route skip the ball to the next character within the rotation.

First, this instills thoughtfulness earlier than movement. Catching the ball is the preliminary reaction, the idea. Choosing who to throw it to represents the belief, and the toss is their motion. It can also display, as exclusive video video video games have already achieved, which pairs inside the circle of relatives have the most powerful bonds and which the weakest. Use your very very own growing emotional intelligence to decipher why that is and the way you may lightly have an effect on it.

The activity is as smooth as that. But you may make it more hard in the following '2d spherical'...

Let every holder of the ball accept as true with a small trick they are capable of do with the ball, then announce it. After doing the trick, the child proclaims the man or woman whom they've chosen to skip the ball to. Such easy and fun guidelines embody matters the very younger can do:

•Turn around

•Touch the ground

•Touch the pinnacle of the top

•Rub the belly

STOP AND TOSS

If you're gambling this with older children and extra more youthful, you'll need to allow the older children do extra complicated recommendations, some of which might be:

•Weaving the ball via the legs

•Looping the ball around the again

•Raising the ball over the pinnacle

• Bouncing it on pinnacle of the pinnacle

• Bouncing the ball (if the ball will soar)

Note what recommendations they select, and what form of physical dexterity they show off.

Also take be conscious within the event that they continuously pass it to themselves masses, as this could display screen early signs and symptoms of isolation, loneliness, or narcissistic and delinquent tendencies. It's continuously appropriate to entice matters early, so ask them how they will be feeling that day. The recreation can emerge as a beneficial precursor to a honestly critical verbal exchange.

Keep the game advancing with the useful resource of letting children do pointers earlier than passing the ball. Encourage them to make up their very own hints. Enjoy their alternatives and praise them with laughter and assist. Always snicker with them and in no way at them, of path.

Stop And Toss, Emotional Edition:

This one is probably higher for slightly older children, however do permit your more youthful kids the risk to attempt. You is probably surprised what they arrive up with! Follow the equal policies for Stop and Toss. Only this time, in preference to doing any tips with the ball, have the kids designate an emotion to the ball, and then enact that emotion. As the sport chief, you start with an instance.

Pick 'worry' and then direct worry at the ball. Toss it up and recoil, make a hectic face and shriek in fear. Be exaggerated and comical, illicit as a notable deal enthusiasm as you may. Then decide who you'll toss the ball to, and toss it. Let the following man or woman choose out their very personal emotion, then reveal it, then they pick the following person (an crucial element) and pass the ball.

Note who chooses what type of emotion. What does it show about their development (and this may be your or your partner or associate as a top notch deal as any of the youngsters)? Make certain to guide the game, which include exceptional emotions inside the event that they appear to be missing. If they're, what does that mean approximately the us of your circle of relatives? Is there too much terrible emotion in your private home? Why? Who brings that into the residence? You? If so, you understand you want to take some notable motion to change that situation.

To venture your youngsters' reminiscence (and your very own) strive combining each games. First, the child or decide catches the ball, they name an emotion and enact it, then do a trick, then pick out someone to pass the ball to. Like Simon and such a number of one-of-a-kind video games, this can enhance them intellectually even as they play. It moreover sincerely encourages the bond amongst

emotionality and thoughts, and that's foremost to emotional intelligence.

If any of the game lovers forget about to do one or the opportunity (omitting an emotion/enactment or a trick), permit them to bypass a flip. Mistakes and mishandling of the cycle of conduct have outcomes, and that may be a superb manner to analyze that. Don't be too difficult on them, even though. Allow them to have a few quality institutions with failure. It's part of the device of achievement, and you may remind them of that.

Backyard Soup:

This is a laugh exercise for more youthful youngsters, ladies specifically. It's wonderful for severa youngsters, so if your infant is having a playdate or if you have numerous youngsters, try and whip up a batch of this tasty confection!

Simply determine you'll be making some outside soup. You can prepare a listing of not unusual history devices you could use, along with:

•Rocks

•Pebbles

•Sticks

•Leaves

•Grass

Chapter 14: Games for Preteens (Ages eight-12)

As children grow antique, they're extra perceptive and more expressive, and their comprehension abilties flourish. At this degree of the cycle of conduct, they may be although extra frequently than now not creatures of emotion, however idea will become more vital to their movements. The video video video games on this chapter are designed to growth the decision for upon decoding feelings, and people video video games moreover begin to teach the skills required for lively listening.

Freaky Friday:

You can also apprehend the story trope of a body switch, regularly among decide and little one. If you've in no way visible any model of this movie or its derivations, it's normally a lightning bolt or curse or a few component which, in this situation, locations the awareness of the child into the body of the parent and the recognition of the discern into the frame of the child. Each need to live lifestyles through the opportunity's mindset, reading empathy along the way.

Well, there's little reason you may't do that at the side of your preteens and more younger teens. Some older young adults may also moreover even be inclined to play along, but they're already in a strange transitional period among early life and adulthood, just so they lack the important physical assessment which makes this test impactful. Even so, they'll be able to frame-trade with a younger sibling.

This is some thing you may do over the dinner table. A lot of those video video games are suitable for such gatherings, because of the reality that's one of the few instances that you have anybody already collected around the table. You have to talk about some thing other than what they decided out in college that day, in any case. Not that you don't want to invite that, but dinner is prolonged.

So, strive having a conversation in that you're the child and your teenager is the decide. You don't have to anticipate a infantile voice (I in my view recommend in competition to it), even though your little one can and likely will expect an person voice and way. You can have an effect on your manner a piece, however undergo in thoughts which you don't need to move away your little one with a long-lasting effect. Don't allow them to enjoy that they're being mocked or aped, or that you are. You don't need your little one to peer you as lots lots much less than an authoritative determine ultimately, however a laugh a transient feature-reversal take a look at might be.

Gear the communication towards circle of relatives topics. The concept of this take a look at is as a way to look the arena thru any person else's eyes, everybody whose life is comparable but one-of-a-type out of your personal. Parents and youngsters fit this bill perfectly.

So as the kid, ask your determine approximately their person worries. Give them a taste of what it's like on your global. Ask approximately subjects from your private art work, even the demanding topics. Ask them for recommendation on your very private dealings on the schoolyard. Tease them (best a little) with a number of the topics they will do to bother you. It's a excellent way to create empathy, to generate the functionality to percentage a top notch attitude, and perhaps even lightly decrease your children's behavior in some techniques.

It will also be revealing about what type of instance you're setting. If you pay attention to their solutions, you'll see their variations of you, their visions of you. Are they callous towards others after they relate recollections again to the family? Do they make quite a few crude jokes? They're retaining a mirror as tons as you. Knowing that could be a big a part of your private emotional intelligence.

Be careful with this workout. You're still the authority. If some thing, this sport need to pressure that thing domestic. In trying to be the authority, your children ought to get a quick idea of the way hard that may be. If you have got got a couple of infant and that they're swapping roles, don't allow them to mock each different overmuch. Don't allow matters become worse. You can also trade roles in the middle of the sport.

After the sport, don't neglect to talk approximately the game. What did the kids examine? What did you studies? Always lead by using the use of the usage of instance and proportion first. It can also take a hint prodding, however digesting and expertise the instructions being found out is vital. Sure, it's all fun and video games,

till ...

Dragon Brain:

Here's a similar game, although it's quite a chunk extra complex. The dragon, if one ever existed, ought to have had a mind about the dimensions of a walnut. So accumulate the own family anyplace can be on hand and spacious, a dwelling room or own family room. It's actual for outside too, and proper for preteens because of the reality they're regularly into dragons.

Get a walnut (earlier) and sincerely hand it to at least one family member. That man or woman becomes a dragon. Let them skip around the house as a dragon for a while, 5 mins or so. Have them cross again to the family and skip decrease lower back the dragon mind/walnut to the circle of relatives and hand it to everyone else. How extended has it been because you've had license to act like a dragon? Will you be the comical dragon from Shrek, or the little guy from Doc McStuffins, or King Ghidorah from the Godzilla movies?

The amusing a part of this function-play hobby is that the opportunity own family contributors enact the roles of the townspeople. How do they react? There's severa enacted emotion on this pastime, and no actual-worldwide warfare. It teaches youngsters that terrific moves, super or unfriendly, have a right away connection to emotional reactions. The interconnectedness of these things is vital to studying emotional intelligence.

And talking of monsters …

What's My Monster?:

Here's a fun mixture of processes which need

to appeal to older tweens. It's a great one for the dinner table. Keep your dragon mind walnut accessible and bypass it to the most possibly participant. They are to anticipate the man or woman of a famous dragon. They'll know heaps of them. Without announcing what monster they will be, have them describe themselves through the usage of traits. The others, contestants in the sport (if you could), ask questions as a way to assist them recognize which dragon you are. Each questioner have to go through in mind the answers as clues to the solution. Let them beautify their hand to be decided on. It's a fun new twist on What's My Line? And what toddler isn't keen on that antique TV display called What's my line? The idea proper proper right here changed into that someone defined their career (or line, within the old style slang). Questioners ought to deduce someone's career through a series of questions.

Whoever guesses efficiently gets to be the following dragon. Popular dragons may also additionally include:

•King Ghidorah

•Smaug

•Mushu

•Dragonite

•Toothless

•and so forth.

The listing is frightfully prolonged, I'm afraid. Parents may additionally have a difficult time maintaining up with this undertaking with out a piece internet research earlier. Okay, proper right here's an answer key:

•Shenron (Dragon Ball)

•Dragonite (Pokemon)

•Smaug (The Hobbit, Lord of the Rings)

•Viserion (Game of Thrones)

•Haku (Spirited Away)

•King Ghidorah (Godzilla)

•Toothless (How to Train Your Dragon)

•Mushu (Mulan)

Another rule, but, is which you can't ask what movie or e-book they appeared in. It is with the useful useful resource of trait which you find out the man or woman, thru backstory.

So keep the questions targeted on why the dragon is the manner they may be, humorous or in love or scary or indignant. The thinking will direct the sport.

Telephone:

Here's a bona fide traditional (plenty of the ones games are based on classics, which I'm exceptional you've determined). This is also a tremendous exercise in energetic listening, this is a staple of emotional intelligence. Several of our games will recognition in this, so that is a superb one to do early on.

For folks who don't recognize, right here's how the sport is played: The interest leader whispers a word into one person's ear. Let's say, "The turtle and the hare had a race via the woods, however the hare had different things in thoughts." The first player, a toddler, repeats the sentence to the great in their capacity. The 2nd player does the same to the 0.33, and so on. The concept is that the word modifications from one man or woman to the subsequent. By the give up of the road, the two phrases are as compared for the divergence of the proper to the very last.

Good fun.

You do want some humans to do it, but. The more the merrier. Play it as you can any normal version of Telephone. For the ones talents, you as the game chief may pick out to embody emotion references within the sentence. Then pay particular interest to how those terms in particular trade. You may probably discover they come to be exaggerated due to the fact the sentence is surpassed along. Here are some examples to get you started out:

•Mary have turn out to be unhappy that her canine ran away.

•Johnny modified into happy because of the truth he were given a bike for his birthday.

•Peter have become embarrassed at the same time as he fell at the playground.

•Dylan have become proud whilst he acquired the spelling bee.

Coloring Emotions, Preteen Edition:

Kids develop resourceful inclinations early, however they growth those abilties as they age. So have interaction inside the identical exercise as in advance than. But this time, alternatively of choosing one emotion and having your children choose out their shade to represent it, have them select the emotion they'd like to draw. They're older now, capable of making that sort of preference.

So, sit there and draw your feelings. Let the colours aggregate, using something colorations or strokes or styles appear appropriate. Use this time, as you probably did earlier than, to speak approximately what emotions they selected to color and why, what topics may be taking place in their lives as they draw the feelings they're expressing. This is a tried-and-right method of the speakme treatment regularly called artwork therapy.

Now you've all created every different precis difficulty, or a sky. But in choice to stopping right right here, and in preference to moving right now to three other emotion, you're going to draw a foreground to healthful the emotional statistics. Let absolutely everyone use black to attract the foreground, a legitimate creative format. What they draw, of course, is as a great deal as them. In brand new, you're growing a skyscape, so your bodily items, the Earth and something functions it offers, can be along the bottom line of the web page, occupying the lowest region of the internet page. Start from the bottom and maintain it clean.

The difficulty in the foreground also can encompass:

- Trees in a discipline

- Mountains

- A cityscape

- Houses in a suburb

- Farms

- Lonely highways

- People

What subjects the artists pick will possibly mirror strongly on in which their mindset is. The entire photograph might be to reveal masses approximately in which the artist's emotional head is at, in case you'll pardon that expression. Is it a lonely farmhouse in competition to a raging pink sky? Is it a tranquil boat toward a moderate-blue area? Ask your kids what they're drawing and why, what emotions inspired them. Ask them if there are any narratives or stories behind the gadgets they're drawing. Who lives in that farmhouse? How do they enjoy? Why? Who is in that boat, the ones houses? What are they feeling and why?

This sharpens their connections amongst emotions and their motives, and the vicinity of cause amidst it all. Don't worry if neither of you could see any deeper significance in a few trouble you or they've got drawn; rather, you would probably emerge as simply having a giggle approximately it! Any communique collectively along with your children--deep or in any other case--is notwithstanding the fact that courting-building.

Mad Libs, Emotional Edition:

You can pick up any duplicate of Mad Libs or write your very very own. Then fill the story in with congregations of emotion phrases. Every noun want to be an emotion, every verb, each adverb and adjective (which are frequently emotions besides).